The Breadwinner

Deborah Ellis

D1450732

OXFORD
UNIVERSITY PRESS

OXFORD
UNIVERSITY PRESS

Great Clarendon Street, Oxford OX2 6DP

Oxford University Press is a department of the University of Oxford.
It furthers the University's objective of excellence in research, scholarship,
and education by publishing worldwide in

Oxford   New York

Auckland   Cape Town   Dar es Salaam   Hong Kong   Karachi
Kuala Lumpur   Madrid   Melbourne   Mexico City   Nairobi
New Delhi   Shanghai   Taipei   Toronto

With offices in

Argentina   Austria   Brazil   Chile   Czech Republic   France   Greece
Guatemala   Hungary   Italy   Japan   Poland   Portugal   Singapore
South Korea   Switzerland   Thailand   Turkey   Ukraine   Vietnam

Oxford is a registered trade mark of Oxford University Press
in the UK and in certain other countries

Database right Oxford University Press (maker)

First published 2000

This educational edition first published 2010

British Library Cataloguing in Publication Data

Data available

ISBN 978-0-19-832980-0

3 5 7 9 10 8 6 4

Printed by Printplus, China

To the children of war

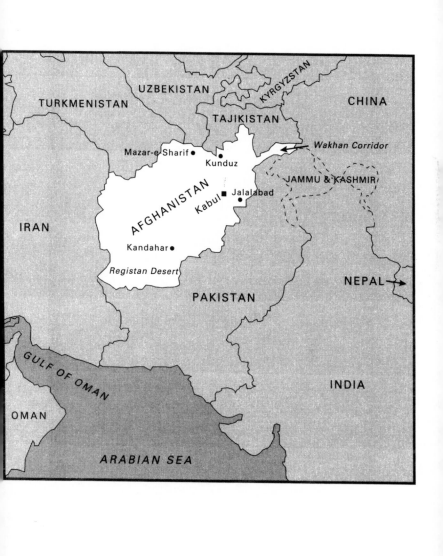

ONE

"I can read that letter as well as Father can," Parvana whispered into the folds of her chador. "Well, almost."

She didn't dare say those words out loud. The man sitting beside her father would not want to hear her voice. Nor would anyone else in the Kabul market. Parvana was there only to help her father walk to the market and back home again after work. She sat well back on the blanket, her head and most of her face covered by her chador.

She wasn't really supposed to be outside at all. The Taliban had ordered all the girls and women in Afghanistan to stay inside their homes. They even forbade girls to go to school. Parvana had had to leave her sixth grade class, and her sister Nooria was not allowed to go to her high school. Their mother had been kicked out of her job as a writer for a Kabul radio station. For more than a year now, they had all been stuck inside one room, along with five-year-old Maryam and two-year-old Ali.

Parvana did get out for a few hours most days to help her father walk. She was always glad to go outside, even though it meant sitting for hours on a blanket spread over the hard ground of the marketplace. At least it was something to do. She had even got used to holding her tongue and hiding her face.

She was small for her eleven years. As a small girl, she could usually get away with being outside without being questioned.

"I need this girl to help me walk," her father would tell any Talib who asked, pointing to his leg. He had lost the lower part of his leg when the high school he was teaching in was bombed. His insides had been hurt somehow, too. He was often tired.

"I have no son at home, except for an infant," he would explain. Parvana would slump down further on the blanket and try to make herself look smaller. She was afraid to look up at the soldiers. She had seen what they did, especially to women, the way they would whip and beat someone they thought should be punished.

Sitting in the marketplace day after day, she had seen a lot. When the Taliban were around, what she wanted most of all was to be invisible.

Now the customer asked her father to read his letter again. "Read it slowly, so that I can remember it for my family."

Parvana would have liked to get a letter. Mail delivery had recently started again in Afghanistan, after years of being disrupted by war. Many of her friends had fled the country with their families. She thought they were in Pakistan, but she wasn't sure, so she couldn't write to them. Her own family had moved so often because of the bombing that her friends no longer knew where she was. "Afghans cover the earth like stars cover the sky," her father often said.

Her father finished reading the man's letter a second time. The customer thanked him and paid. "I will look for you when it is time to write a reply."

Most people in Afghanistan could not read or write. Parvana was one of the lucky ones. Both of her parents had been to university, and they believed in education for everyone, even girls.

Customers came and went as the afternoon wore on. Most spoke Dari, the same language Parvana spoke best. When a customer spoke Pashtu, she could recognize most of it, but not all. Her parents could speak English, too. Her father had gone to university in England. That was a long time ago.

The market was a very busy place. Men shopped for their families, and peddlers hawked their goods and services. Some, like the tea shop, had their own stalls. With such a big urn and so many trays of cups, it had to stay in one place. Tea boys ran back and forth into the labyrinth of the marketplace, carrying tea to customers who couldn't leave their own shops, then running back again with the empty cups.

"I could do that," Parvana whispered. She'd like to be able to run around in the market, to know its winding streets as well as she knew the four walls of her home.

Her father turned to look at her. "I'd rather see you running around a school yard." He turned around again to call out to the passing men. "Anything written! Anything read! Pashtu and Dari! Wonderful items for sale!"

Parvana frowned. It wasn't her fault she

wasn't in school! She would rather be there, too, instead of sitting on this uncomfortable blanket, her back and bottom getting sore. She missed her friends, her blue-and-white school uniform, and doing new things each day.

History was her favorite subject, especially Afghan history. Everybody had come to Afghanistan. The Persians came four thousand years ago. Alexander the Great came, too, followed by the Greeks, Arabs, Turks, British, and finally the Soviets. One of the conquerors, Tamerlane from Samarkand, cut off the heads of his enemies and stacked them in huge piles, like melons at a fruit stand. All these people had come to Parvana's beautiful country to try to take it over, and the Afghans had kicked them all out again!

But now the country was ruled by the Taliban militia. They were Afghans, and they had very definite ideas about how things should be run. When they first took over the capital city of Kabul and forbade girls to go to school, Parvana wasn't terribly unhappy. She had a test coming up in arithmetic that she hadn't prepared for, and she was in trouble for talking in class again. The teacher was going to send a note to her mother, but the Taliban took over first.

"What are you crying for?" she had asked Nooria, who couldn't stop sobbing. "I think a holiday is very nice." Parvana was sure the Taliban would let them go back to school in a few days. By then her teacher would have forgotten all about sending a tattletale note to her mother.

"You're just stupid!" Nooria screamed at her. "Leave me alone!"

One of the difficulties of living with your whole family in one room was that it was impossible to really leave anyone alone. Wherever Nooria went, there was Parvana. And wherever Parvana went, there was Nooria.

Both of Parvana's parents had come from old respected Afghan families. With their education, they had earned high salaries. They had had a big house with a courtyard, a couple of servants, a television set, a refrigerator, a car. Nooria had had her own room. Parvana had shared a room with her little sister, Maryam. Maryam chattered a lot, but she thought Parvana was wonderful. It had certainly been wonderful to get away from Nooria sometimes.

That house had been destroyed by a bomb. The family had moved several times since then. Each time, they moved to a smaller place. Every time their house was bombed, they lost more of their things. With each bomb, they got poorer. Now they lived together in one small room.

There had been a war going on in Afghanistan for more than twenty years, twice as long as Parvana had been alive.

At first it was the Soviets who rolled their big tanks into the country and flew war planes that dropped bombs on villages and the countryside.

Parvana was born one month before the Soviets started going back to their own country.

"You were such an ugly baby, the Soviets couldn't stand to be in the same country with you," Nooria was fond of telling her. "They fled back across the border in horror, as fast as their tanks could carry them."

After the Soviets left, the people who had been shooting at the Soviets decided they wanted to keep shooting at something, so they shot at each other. Many bombs fell on Kabul during that time. Many people died.

Bombs had been part of Parvana's whole life. Every day, every night, rockets would fall out of the sky, and someone's house would explode.

When the bombs fell, people ran. First they ran one way, then they ran another, trying to find a place where the bombs wouldn't find them. When she was younger, Parvana was carried. When she got bigger, she had to do her own running.

Now most of the country was controlled by the Taliban. The word Taliban meant religious students, but Parvana's father told her that religion was about teaching people how to be better human beings, how to be kinder. "The Taliban are not making Afghanistan a kinder place to live!" he said.

Although bombs still fell on Kabul, they didn't fall as often as they used to. There was still a war going on in the north of the country, and that was where most of the killing took place these days.

After a few more customers had come and gone, Father suggested they end their work for the day.

Parvana jumped to her feet, then collapsed

back down again. Her foot was asleep. She rubbed it, then tried again. This time she was able to stand.

First she gathered up all the little items they were trying to sell—dishes, pillow cases, household ornaments that had survived the bombings. Like many Afghans, they sold what they could. Mother and Nooria regularly went through what was left of the family's belongings to see what they could spare. There were so many people selling things in Kabul, Parvana marveled that there was anyone left to buy them.

Father packed his pens and writing paper in his shoulder bag. Leaning on his walking stick and taking Parvana's arm, he slowly stood up. Parvana shook the dust out of the blanket, folded it up, and they were on their way.

For short distances Father could manage with just his walking stick. For longer journeys he needed Parvana to lean on.

"You're just the right height," he said.

"What will happen when I grow?"

"Then I will grow with you!"

Father used to have a false leg, but he sold it. He hadn't planned to. False legs had to be specially made, and one person's false leg didn't necessarily fit another. But when a customer saw Father's leg on the blanket, he ignored the other things for sale and demanded to buy the leg. He offered such a good price that Father eventually relented.

There were a lot of false legs for sale in the market now. Since the Taliban decreed that women must stay inside, many husbands took their wives' false legs away. "You're not going anywhere, so why do you need a leg?" they asked.

There were bombed-out buildings all over Kabul. Neighborhoods had turned from homes and businesses into bricks and dust.

Kabul had once been beautiful. Nooria remembered whole sidewalks, traffic lights that changed color, evening trips to restaurants and cinemas, browsing in fine shops for clothes and books.

For most of Parvana's life, the city had been in ruins, and it was hard for her to imagine it another way. It hurt her to hear stories of old Kabul before the bombing. She didn't want to think about everything the bombs had taken away, including her father's health and their beautiful home. It made her angry, and since she could do nothing with her anger, it made her sad.

They left the busy part of the market and turned down a side street to their building. Parvana carefully guided her father around the pot holes and broken places in the road.

"How do women in burqas manage to walk along these streets?" Parvana asked her father. "How do they see where they are going?"

"They fall down a lot," her father replied. He was right. Parvana had seen them fall.

She looked at her favorite mountain. It rose up majestically at the end of her street.

"What's the name of that mountain?" she had asked her father soon after they moved to their new neighborhood.

"That's Mount Parvana."

"It is not," Nooria had said scornfully.

"You shouldn't lie to the child," Mother had said. The whole family had been out walking together, in the time before the Taliban. Mother and Nooria just wore light scarves around their hair. Their faces soaked up the Kabul sunshine.

"Mountains are named by people," Father

said. "I am a person, and I name that mountain Mount Parvana."

Her mother gave in, laughing. Father laughed, too, and Parvana and baby Maryam, who didn't even know why she was laughing. Even grumpy Nooria joined in. The sound of the family's laughter scampered up Mount Parvana and back down into the street.

Now Parvana and her father slowly made their way up the steps of their building. They lived on the third floor of an apartment building. It had been hit in a rocket attack, and half of it was rubble.

The stairs were on the outside of the building, zigzagging back and forth on their way up. They had been damaged by the bomb, and didn't quite meet in places. Only some parts of the staircase had a railing. "Never rely on the railing," Father told Parvana over and over. Going up was easier for Father than going down, but it still took a long time.

Finally they reached the door of their home and went inside.

TWO

Mother and Nooria were cleaning again. Father kissed Ali and Maryam, went to the bathroom to wash the dust off his foot, face and hands, then stretched out on a toshak for a rest.

Parvana put down her bundles and started to take off her chador.

"We need water," Nooria said.

"Can't I sit down for awhile first?" Parvana asked her mother.

"You will rest better when your work is done. Now go. The water tank is almost empty."

Parvana groaned. If the tank was almost empty, she'd have to make five trips to the water tap. Six, because her mother hated to see an empty water bucket.

"If you had fetched it yesterday, when Mother asked you, you wouldn't have so much to haul today," Nooria said as Parvana passed by her to get to the water bucket. Nooria smiled her superior big-sister smile and flipped her hair back over her shoulders. Parvana wanted to kick her.

Nooria had beautiful hair, long and thick. Parvana's hair was thin and stringy. She wanted hair like her sister's, and Nooria knew this.

Parvana grumbled all the way down the steps and down the block to the neighborhood tap. The trip home, with a full bucket, was worse, especially the three flights of stairs. Being angry at Nooria gave her the energy to do it, so Parvana kept grumbling.

"Nooria never goes for water, nor does Mother. Maryam doesn't, either. She doesn't have to do anything!"

Parvana knew she was mumbling nonsense, but she kept it up anyway. Maryam was only five, and she couldn't carry an empty bucket downstairs, let alone a full bucket upstairs. Mother and Nooria had to wear burqas whenever they went outside, and they couldn't carry a pail of water up those uneven broken stairs if they were wearing burqas. Plus, it was dangerous for women to go outside without a man.

Parvana knew she had to fetch the water

because there was nobody else in the family who could do it. Sometimes this made her resentful. Sometimes it made her proud. One thing she knew—it didn't matter how she felt. Good mood or bad, the water had to be fetched, and she had to fetch it.

Finally the tank was full, the water bucket was full, and Parvana could slip off her sandals, hang up her chador and relax. She sat on the floor beside Maryam and watched her little sister draw a picture.

"You're very talented, Maryam. One day you will sell your drawings for tons and tons of money. We will be very rich and live in a palace, and you will wear blue silk dresses."

"Green silk," Maryam said.

"Green silk," Parvana agreed.

"Instead of just sitting there, you could help us over here." Mother and Nooria were cleaning out the cupboard again.

"You cleaned out the cupboard three days ago!"

"Are you going to help us or not?"

Not, Parvana thought, but she got to her feet. Mother and Nooria were always cleaning something. Since they couldn't work or go to school, they didn't have much else to do. "The Taliban have said we must stay inside, but that doesn't mean we have to live in filth," Mother was fond of saying.

Parvana hated all that cleaning. It used up the water she had to haul. The only thing worse was for Nooria to wash her hair.

Parvana looked around their tiny room. All of the furniture she remembered from their other houses had been destroyed by bombs or stolen by looters. All they had now was a tall wooden cupboard, which had been in the room when they rented it. It held the few belongings they had been able to save. Two toshaks were set against the walls, and that was all the furniture they had. They used to have beautiful Afghan carpets. Parvana remembered tracing the intricate patterns of them with her fingers when she was younger. Now there was just cheap matting over the cement floor.

Parvana could cross their main room with ten regular steps one way and twelve regular steps the other way. It was usually her job to sweep the mat with their tiny whisk broom. She knew every inch of it.

At the end of the room was the lavatory. It

was a very small room with a platform toilet—not the modern Western toilet they used to have! The little propane cookstove was kept in there because a tiny vent, high in the wall, kept fresh air coming into the room. The water tank was there, too—a metal drum that held five pails of water—and the wash basin was next to that.

Other people lived in the part of the building that was still standing. Parvana saw them as she went to fetch water or went out with her father to the marketplace. "We must keep our distance," Father told her. "The Taliban encourage neighbor to spy on neighbor. It is safer to keep to ourselves."

It may have been safer, Parvana often thought, but it was also lonely. Maybe there was another girl her age, right close by, but she'd never find out. Father had his books, Maryam played with Ali, Nooria had Mother, but Parvana didn't have anybody.

Mother and Nooria had wiped down the cupboard shelves. Now they were putting things back.

"Here is a pile of things for your father to sell in the market. Put them by the door," Mother directed her.

The vibrant red cloth caught Parvana's eye. "My good shalwar kameez! We can't sell that!"

"I decide what we're going to sell, not you. There's no longer any use for it, unless you're planning to go to parties you haven't bothered to tell me about."

Parvana knew there was no point arguing. Ever since she had been forced out of her job, Mother's temper grew shorter every day.

Parvana put the outfit with the other items by the door. She ran her fingers over the intricate embroidery. It had been an Eid present from her aunt in Mazar-e-Sharif, a city in the north of Afghanistan. She hoped her aunt would be angry at her mother for selling it.

"Why don't we sell Nooria's good clothes? She's not going anywhere."

"She'll need them when she gets married."

Nooria made a superior sort of face at Parvana. As an extra insult, she tossed her head to make her long hair swing.

"I pity whoever marries you," Parvana said. "He will be getting a stuck-up snob for a wife."

"That's enough," Mother said.

Parvana fumed. Mother always took Nooria's side. Parvana hated Nooria, and she'd hate her mother, too, if she wasn't her mother.

Her anger melted when she saw her mother pick up the parcel of Hossain's clothes and put it away on the top shelf of the cupboard. Her mother always looked sad when she touched Hossain's clothes.

Nooria hadn't always been the oldest. Hossain had been the oldest child. He had been killed by a land mine when he was fourteen years old. Mother and Father never talked about him. To remember him was too painful. Nooria had told Parvana about him during one of the rare times they were talking to each other.

Hossain had laughed a lot, and was always trying to get Nooria to play games with him, even though she was a girl. "Don't be such a princess," he'd say. "A little football will do you good!" Sometimes, Nooria said, she'd give in and play, and Hossain would always kick the ball to her in a way that she could stop it and kick it back.

"He used to pick you up and play with you a lot," Nooria told Parvana. "He actually seemed to like you. Imagine that!"

From Nooria's stories, Hossain sounded like

someone Parvana would have liked, too.

Seeing the pain in her mother's face, Parvana put her anger away and quietly helped get supper ready.

The family ate Afghan-style, sitting around a plastic cloth spread out on the floor. Food cheered everyone up, and the family lingered after the meal was over.

At some point, Parvana knew, a secret signal would pass between her mother and Nooria, and the two of them would rise at the same instant to begin clearing up. Parvana had no idea how they did it. She would watch for a sign to go between the two of them, but she could never see one.

Ali was dozing on Mother's lap, a piece of nan in his little fist. Every now and then he would realize he was falling asleep and would rouse himself, as if he hated the thought of missing something. He'd try to get up, but Mother held him quite firmly. After wiggling for a moment, he'd give up and doze off again.

Father, looking rested after his nap, had changed into his good white shalwar kameez. His long beard was neatly combed. Parvana thought he looked very handsome.

When the Taliban first came and ordered all men to grow beards, Parvana had a hard time getting used to her father's face. He had never worn a beard before. Father had a hard time getting used to it, too. It itched a lot at first.

Now he was telling stories from history. He had been a history teacher before his school was bombed. Parvana had grown up with his stories, which made her a very good student in history class.

"It was 1880, and the British were trying to take over our country. Did we want the British to take over?" he asked Maryam.

"No!" Maryam answered.

"We certainly did not. Everybody comes to Afghanistan to try to take over, but we Afghans kick them all out. We are the most welcoming, hospitable people on earth. A guest to us is a king. You girls remember that. When a guest comes to your house, he must have the best of everything."

"Or she," Parvana said.

Father grinned at her. "Or she. We Afghans do everything we can to make our guest comfortable. But if someone comes into our home or our country and acts like our enemy, then we will defend our home."

"Father, get on with the story," Parvana urged. She had heard it before, many times, but she wanted to hear it again.

Father grinned again. "We must teach this child some patience," he said to Mother. Parvana didn't need to look at her mother to know she was probably thinking they needed to teach her a whole lot more than that.

"All right," he relented. "On with the story. It was 1880. In the dust around the city of Kandahar, the Afghans were fighting the British. It was a terrible battle. Many were dead. The British were winning, and the Afghans were ready to give up. Their spirits were low, they had no strength to keep fighting. Surrender and capture were starting to look good to them. At least they could rest and maybe save their lives.

"Suddenly a tiny girl, younger than Nooria, burst out from one of the village houses. She ran to the front of the battle and turned to face the Afghan troops. She ripped the veil off her head, and with the hot sun streaming down on her face and her bare head, she called to the troops.

"'We can win this battle!' she cried. 'Don't give up hope! Pick yourselves up! Let's go!' Waving her veil in the air like a battle flag, she led the troops into a final rush at the British. The British had no chance. The Afghans won the battle.

"The lesson here, my daughters," he looked from one to the other, "is that Afghanistan has always been the home of the bravest women in the world. You are all brave women. You are all inheritors of the courage of Malali."

"We can win this battle!" Maryam cried out, waving her arm around as if she were holding a flag. Mother moved the tea pot out of harm's way.

"How can we be brave?" Nooria asked. "We can't even go outside. How can we lead men into battle? I've seen enough war. I don't want to see any more."

"There are many types of battles," Father said quietly.

"Including the battle with the supper dishes," Mother said.

Parvana made such a face that Father started to laugh. Maryam tried to imitate it, which made Mother and Nooria laugh. Ali woke up, saw everybody laughing, and he started to laugh, too.

The whole family was laughing when four Taliban soldiers burst through the door.

Ali was the first to react. The slam of the door against the wall shocked him, and he screamed.

Mother leapt to her feet, and in an instant Ali and Maryam were in a corner of the room, shrieking behind her legs.

Nooria covered herself completely with her chador and scrunched herself into a small ball. Young women were sometimes stolen by soldiers. They were snatched from their homes, and their families never saw them again.

Parvana couldn't move. She sat as if frozen at the edge of the supper cloth. The soldiers were giants, their piled-high turbans making them look even taller.

Two of the soldiers grabbed her father. The other two began searching the apartment, kicking the remains of dinner all over the mat.

"Leave him alone!" Mother screamed. "He has done nothing wrong!"

"Why did you go to England for your education?" the soldiers yelled at Father. "Afghanistan doesn't need your foreign ideas!" They yanked him toward the door.

"Afghanistan needs more illiterate thugs like you," Father said. One of the soldiers hit him in the face. Blood from his nose dripped onto his white shalwar kameez.

Mother sprang at the soldiers, pounding them with her fists. She grabbed Father's arm and tried to pull him out of their grasp.

One of the soldiers raised his rifle and whacked her on the head. She collapsed on the floor. The soldier hit her a few more times. Maryam and Ali screamed with every blow to their mother's back.

Seeing her mother on the ground finally propelled Parvana into action. When the soldiers dragged her father outside, she flung her arms around his waist. As the soldiers pried her loose, she heard her father say, "Take care of the others, my Malali." Then he was gone.

Parvana watched helplessly as two soldiers dragged him down the steps, his beautiful shalwar kameez ripping on the rough cement. Then they turned a corner, and she could see them no more.

Inside the room, the other two soldiers were ripping open the toshaks with knives and tossing things out of the cupboard.

Father's books! At the bottom of the cupboard was a secret compartment her father had built to hide the few books that had not been destroyed in one of the bombings. Some were English books about history and literature. They were kept hidden because the Taliban burned books they didn't like.

They couldn't be allowed to find Father's books! The soldiers had started at the top of the cupboard and were working their way down. Clothes, blankets, pots—everything landed on the floor.

Closer and closer they came to the bottom shelf, the one with the false wall. Parvana watched in horror as the soldiers bent down to yank the things out of the bottom shelf.

"Get out of my house!" she yelled. She threw herself at the soldiers with such force that they both fell to the ground. She swung at them with her fists until she was knocked aside. She heard rather than felt the thwack of their sticks on her back. She kept her head hidden in her arms until the beating stopped and the soldiers went away.

Mother got off the floor and had her hands full with Ali. Nooria was still curled up in a terrified ball. It was Maryam who came over to help Parvana.

At the first touch of her sister's hands, Parvana flinched, thinking it was the soldiers. Maryam kept stroking her hair until Parvana realized who it was. She sat up, aching all over. She and Maryam clung to each other, trembling.

She had no idea how long the family stayed like that. They remained in their spots long after Ali stopped screaming and collapsed into sleep.

THREE

Mother gently placed the sleeping Ali on an uncluttered spot on the floor. Maryam had fallen asleep, too, and was carried over to sleep beside her brother.

"Let's clean up," Mother said. Slowly, they put the room back together. Parvana's back and legs ached. Mother moved slowly, too, all hunched over.

Mother and Nooria replaced things in the cupboard. Parvana got the whisk broom down from its nail in the lavatory and swept up the spilled rice. She wiped up the spilled tea with a cloth. The ripped toshaks could be repaired, but that would wait until tomorrow.

When the room looked somewhat normal again, the family, minus Father, spread quilts and blankets on the floor and went to bed.

Parvana couldn't sleep. She could hear her mother and Nooria tossing and turning as well. She imagined every single noise to be either

Father or the Taliban coming back. Each sound made Parvana hopeful and fearful at the same time.

She missed her father's snoring. He had a soft, pleasant snore. During the heavy bombing of Kabul, they changed homes many times to try to find a safe place. Parvana would wake up in the middle of the night and not remember where she was. As soon as she heard her father's snoring, she knew she was safe.

Tonight, there was no snoring.

Where was her father? Did he have a soft place to sleep? Was he cold? Was he hungry? Was he scared?

Parvana had never been inside a prison, but she had other relatives who had been arrested. One of her aunts had been arrested with hundreds of other schoolgirls for protesting the Soviet occupation of her country. All the Afghan governments put their enemies in jail.

"You can't be truly Afghan if you don't know someone who's been in prison," her mother sometimes said.

No one had told her what prison was like. "You're too young to know these things," the grown-ups would tell her. She had to imagine it.

It would be cold, Parvana decided, and dark.

"Mother, turn on the lamp!" She sat bolt upright with a sudden thought.

"Parvana, hush! You'll wake Ali."

"Light the lamp," Parvana whispered. "If they let Father go, he'll need a light in the window to guide him home."

"How could he walk? He left his walking stick here. Parvana, go to sleep. You are not helping the situation."

Parvana lay down again, but she didn't sleep.

The only window in the room was a small one, high up on one wall. The Taliban had ordered all windows painted over with black paint so that no one could see the women inside. "We won't do it," Father had said. "The window is so high and so small, no one can possibly see in." So far, they had gotten away with leaving it unpainted.

For short periods, on clear days, the sun would come through the window in a thin stream. Ali and Maryam would sit in that ray of sunshine. Mother and Nooria would join them there and, for a few moments, the sun would warm the flesh on their arms and faces. Then the planet would continue its spin, and the sunbeam would be gone again.

Parvana kept her eyes on the spot where she thought the window was. The night was so dark, she could not distinguish between the window and the wall. She kept watch all night, until the dawn finally pushed the darkness away, and morning peeked in through the window.

At first light, Mother, Nooria and Parvana stopped pretending they were asleep. Quietly, so they didn't wake the young ones, they got up and dressed.

For breakfast they chewed on leftover nan. Nooria started to heat water for tea on the little gas stove in the bathroom, but Mother stopped her. "There is boiled water left from last night. We'll just drink that. We don't have time to wait for tea. Parvana and I are going to get your father out of jail." She said it the way she might say, "Parvana and I are going to the market to get peaches."

The nan fell from Parvana's lips onto the plastic cloth. She didn't argue, though.

Maybe I'll get to finally see what the inside of a jail looks like, she thought.

The prison was a long way from their home.

Buses were not permitted to carry women who did not have a man with them. They would have to walk the whole way. What if Father was being held somewhere else? What if they were stopped by the Taliban in the street? Mother wasn't supposed to be out of her home without a man, or without a note from her husband.

"Nooria, write Mother a note."

"Don't bother, Nooria. I will not walk around my own city with a note pinned to my burqa as if I were a kindergarten child. I have a university degree!"

"Write the note anyway," Parvana whispered to Nooria, when Mother was in the washroom. "I'll carry it in my sleeve."

Nooria agreed. Her penmanship was more grown-up than Parvana's. She quickly wrote, "I give permission for my wife to be outside." She signed it with Father's name.

"I don't think it will do much good," Nooria whispered, as she handed Parvana the note. "Most of the Taliban don't know how to read."

Parvana didn't answer. She quickly folded the note into a small square and tucked it into the wide hem of her sleeve.

Nooria suddenly did something very unusual. She gave her sister a hug. "Come back," she whispered.

Parvana didn't want to go, but she knew that sitting at home waiting for them to return would be even harder.

"Hurry up, Parvana," her mother said. "Your father is waiting."

Parvana slipped her feet into her sandals and wound her chador around her head. She followed Mother out the door.

Helping Mother down the broken stairs was a little like helping Father, as the billowing burqa made it hard for her to see where she was going.

Mother hesitated at the bottom of the stairs. Parvana thought she might be having second thoughts. After that moment, though, her mother pulled herself up to her full height, straightened her back and plunged into the Kabul street.

Parvana rushed after her. She had to run to keep up with her mother's long, quick steps, but she didn't dare fall behind. There were a few other women in the street and they all wore the regulation burqa, which made them all look alike. If Parvana lost track of her mother, she was afraid she'd never find her again.

Now and then, her mother stopped beside a man and a woman, or a small group of men, or even a peddler boy, and held out a photograph of Father. She didn't say anything, just showed them the photo.

Parvana held her breath every time her mother did this. Photographs were illegal. Any one of these people could turn Parvana and her mother over to the militia.

But everyone looked at the photo, then shook their heads. Many people had been arrested. Many people had disappeared. They knew what Mother was asking without her having to say anything.

Pul-i-Charkhi Prison was a long walk from Parvana's home. By the time the huge fortress came into view, her legs were sore, her feet ached and, worst of all, she was scared all over.

The prison was dark and ugly, and it made Parvana feel even smaller.

Malali wouldn't be afraid, Parvana knew. Malali would form an army and lead it in a storming of the prison. Malali would lick her lips at such a challenge. Her knees wouldn't be shaking as Parvana's were.

If Parvana's mother was scared, she didn't show it. She marched straight up to the prison gates and said to the guard, "I'm here for my husband."

The guards ignored her.

"I'm here for my husband!" Mother said again. She took out Father's photograph and held it in front of the face of one of the guards. "He was arrested last night. He has committed no crime, and I want him released!"

More guards began to gather. Parvana gave a little tug on her mother's burqa. Her mother ignored her.

"I'm here for my husband!" she kept saying, louder and louder. Parvana tugged harder on the loose cloth of the burqa.

"Hold steady, my little Malali," she heard her father say in her mind. Suddenly, she felt very calm.

"I'm here for my father!" she called out.

Her mother looked down at her through the screen over her eyes. She reached down and took Parvana's hand. "I'm here for my husband!" she called again.

Over and over, Parvana and her mother kept yelling out their mission. More and more men came to stare at them.

"Be quiet!" ordered one of the guards. "You should not be here! Go from this place! Go back to your home!"

One of the soldiers snatched the photo of Parvana's father and tore it into pieces. Another started hitting her mother with a stick.

"Release my husband!" her mother kept saying.

Another soldier joined in the beating. He hit Parvana, too.

Although he did not hit her very hard, Parvana fell to the ground, her body covering the pieces of her father's photograph. In a flash, she tucked the pieces out of sight, under her chador.

Her mother was also on the ground, the soldier's sticks hitting her across her back.

Parvana leapt to her feet. "Stop! Stop it! We'll go now! We'll go!" She grabbed the arm of one of her mother's attackers. He shook her off as if she were a fly.

"Who are you to tell me what to do?" But he did lower his stick.

"Get out of here!" he spat at Parvana and her mother.

Parvana knelt down, took her mother's arm and helped her to her feet. Slowly, with her mother leaning on her for support, they hobbled away from the prison.

FOUR

It was very late by the time Parvana and her
mother returned home from the prison.
Parvana was so tired she had to lean against
Mother to make it up the stairs, the way Father
used to lean against her. She had stopped thinking of anything but the pain that seemed to be
in every part of her body, from the top of her
head to the bottom of her feet.

Her feet burned and stung with every step.
When she took off her sandals, she could see
why. Her feet, unused to walking such long distances, were covered with blisters. Most of the
blisters had broken, and her feet were bloody
and raw.

Nooria and Maryam's eyes widened when
they saw the mess of Parvana's feet. They grew
wider still when they saw their mother's feet.
They were even more torn up and bloody than
Parvana's.

Parvana realized that Mother hadn't been

out of the house since the Taliban had taken over Kabul a year and a half before. She could have gone out. She had a burqa, and Father would have gone with her any time she wanted. Many husbands were happy to make their wives stay home, but not Father.

"Fatana, you are a writer," he often said. "You must come out into the city and see what is happening. Otherwise, how will you know what to write about it?"

"Who would read what I write? Am I allowed to publish? No. Then what is the point of writing, and what is the point of looking? Besides, it will not be for long. The Afghan people are smart and strong. They will kick these Taliban out. When that happens, when we have a decent government in Afghanistan, then I will go out again. Until then, I will stay here."

"It takes work to make a decent government," Father said. "You are a writer. You must do your work."

"If we had left Afghanistan when we had the chance, I could be doing my work!"

"We are Afghans. This is our home. If all the educated people leave, who will rebuild the country?"

It was an argument Parvana's parents had often. When the whole family lived in one room, there were no secrets.

Mother's feet were so bad from the long walk that she could barely make it into the room. Parvana had been so preoccupied with her own pain and exhaustion, she hadn't given any thought to what her mother had been going through.

Nooria tried to help, but Mother just waved her away. She threw her burqa down on the floor. Her face was stained with tears and sweat. She collapsed onto the toshak where Father had taken his nap just yesterday.

Mother cried for a long, long time. Nooria sponged off the part of her face that wasn't buried in the pillow. She washed the dust from the wounds in her mother's feet.

Mother acted as if Nooria wasn't there at all. Finally, Nooria spread a light blanket over her. It was a long time before the sobs stopped, and Mother fell asleep.

While Nooria tried to look after Mother, Maryam looked after Parvana. Biting her tongue in concentration, she carried a basin of water over to where Parvana was sitting. She didn't spill a drop. She wiped Parvana's face with a cloth she wasn't quite able to wring out. Drips from the cloth ran down Parvana's neck. The water felt good. She soaked her feet in the basin, and that felt good, too.

She sat with her feet in the basin while Nooria got supper.

"They wouldn't tell us anything about Father," Parvana told her sister. "What are we going to do? How are we going to find him?"

Nooria started to say something, but Parvana didn't catch what it was. She began to feel heavy, her eyes started to close, and the next thing she knew, it was morning.

Parvana could hear the morning meal being prepared.

I should get up and help, she thought, but she couldn't bring herself to move.

All night long she had drifted in and out of dreams about the soldiers. They were screaming at her and hitting her. In her dream, she shouted at them to release her father, but no sound came from her lips. She had even shouted, "I am Malali! I am Malali!" but the soldiers paid no attention.

The worst part of her dream was seeing

Mother beaten. It was as if Parvana was watching it happen from far, far away, and couldn't get to her to help her up.

Parvana suddenly sat up, then relaxed again when she saw her mother on the toshak on the other side of the room. It was all right. Mother was here.

"I'll help you to the washroom," Nooria offered.

"I don't need any help," Parvana said. However, when she tried to stand, the pain in her feet was very bad. It was easier to accept Nooria's offer and lean on her across the room to the washroom.

"Everybody leans on everybody in this family," Parvana said.

"Is that right?" Nooria asked. "And who do I lean on?"

That was such a Nooria-like comment that Parvana immediately felt a bit better. Nooria being grumpy meant things were getting back to normal.

She felt better still after she'd washed her face and tidied her hair. There was cold rice and hot tea waiting when she had finished.

"Mother, would you like some breakfast?"

Nooria gently shook their mother. Mother moaned a little and shrugged Nooria away.

Except for trips to the washroom, and a couple of cups of tea, which Nooria kept in a thermos by the toshak, Mother spent the day lying down. She kept her face to the wall and didn't speak to any of them.

The next day, Parvana was tired of sleeping. Her feet were still sore, but she played with Ali and Maryam. The little ones, especially Ali, couldn't understand why Mother wasn't paying attention to them.

"Mother's sleeping," Parvana kept saying.

"When will she wake up?" Maryam asked.

Parvana didn't answer.

Ali kept waddling over to the door and pointing up at it.

"I think he's asking where Father is," Nooria said. "Come on, Ali, let's find your ball."

Parvana remembered the pieces of photograph and got them out. Her father's face was like a jigsaw puzzle. She spread the pieces out on the mat in front of her. Maryam joined her and helped her put them in order.

One piece was missing. All of Father's face was there except for a part of his chin. "When we get some tape, we'll tape it together," Parvana said. Maryam nodded. She gathered up the little pieces into a tidy pile and handed them to Parvana. Parvana tucked them away in a corner of the cupboard.

The third day barely creeped along. Parvana even considered doing some housework, just to pass the time, but she was worried she might disturb her mother. At one point, all four children sat against the wall and watched their mother sleep.

"She has to get up soon," Nooria said.

"She can't just lie there forever."

Parvana was tired of sitting. She had lived in that room for a year and a half, but there had always been chores to do and trips to the market with Father.

Mother was still in the same place. They were taking care not to disturb her. All the same, Parvana thought if she had to spend much more time whispering and keeping the young ones quiet, she would scream.

It would help if she could read, but the only books they had were Father's secret books. She didn't dare take them out of their hiding place. What if the Taliban burst in on them again?

They'd take the books, and maybe punish the whole family for having them.

Parvana noticed a change in Ali. "Is he sick?" she asked Nooria.

"He misses Mother." Ali sat in Nooria's lap. He didn't crawl around any more when he was put on the floor. He spent most of the time curled in a ball with his thumb in his mouth.

He didn't even cry very much any more. It was nice to have a break from his noise, but Parvana didn't like to see him like this.

The room began to smell, too. "We have to save water," Nooria said, so washing and cleaning didn't get done. Ali's dirty diapers were piled in a heap in the washroom. The little window didn't open very far. No breeze could get into the room to blow the stink away.

On the fourth day, the food ran out.

"We're out of food," Nooria told Parvana.

"Don't tell me. Tell Mother. She's the grown-up. She has to get us some."

"I don't want to bother her."

"Then I'll tell her." Parvana went over to Mother's toshak and gently shook her.

"We're out of food." There was no response. "Mother, there's no food left." Mother pulled away. Parvana started to shake her again.

"Leave her alone!" Nooria yanked her away. "Can't you see she's depressed?"

"We're all depressed," Parvana replied. "We're also hungry." She wanted to shout, but didn't want to frighten the little ones. She could glare, though, and she and Nooria glared at each other for hours.

No one ate that day.

"We're out of food," Nooria said again to Parvana the next day.

"I'm not going out there."

"You have to go. There's no one else who can go."

"My feet are still sore."

"Your feet will survive, but we won't if you don't get us food. Now, move!"

Parvana looked at Mother, still lying on the toshak. She looked at Ali, worn out from being hungry and needing his parents. She looked at Maryam, whose cheeks were already beginning to look hollow, and who hadn't been in the sunshine in such a long time. Finally, she looked at her big sister, Nooria.

Nooria looked terrified. If Parvana didn't

obey her, she would have to go for food herself.

Now I've got her, Parvana thought. I can make her as miserable as she makes me. But she was surprised to find that this thought gave her no pleasure. Maybe she was too tired and too hungry. Instead of turning her back, she took the money from her sister's hand.

"What should I buy?" she asked.

FIVE

It was strange to be in the marketplace without Father. Parvana almost expected to see him in their usual place, sitting on the blanket, reading and writing his customer's letters.

Women were not allowed to go into the shops. Men were supposed to do all the shopping, but if women did it, they had to stand outside and call in for what they needed. Parvana had seen shopkeepers beaten for serving women inside their shops.

Parvana wasn't sure if she would be considered a woman. On the one hand, if she behaved like one and stood outside the shop and called in her order, she could get in trouble for not wearing a burqa. On the other hand, if she went into a shop, she could get in trouble for not acting like a woman!

She put off her decision by buying the nan first. The baker's stall opened onto the street.

Parvana pulled her chador more tightly

around her face so that only her eyes were showing. She held up ten fingers—ten loaves of nan. A pile of nan was already baked, but she had to wait a little while for four more loaves to be flipped out of the oven. The attendant wrapped the bread in a piece of newspaper and handed it to Parvana. She paid without looking up.

The bread was still warm. It smelled so good! The wonderful smell reminded Parvana how hungry she was. She could have swallowed a whole loaf in one gulp.

The fruit and vegetable stand was next. Before she had time to make a selection, a voice behind her shouted, "What are you doing on the street dressed like that?"

Parvana whirled around to see a Talib glaring at her, anger in his eyes and a stick in his hand.

"You must be covered up! Who is your father? Who is your husband? They will be punished for letting you walk the street like that!" The soldier raised his arm and brought his stick down on Parvana's shoulder.

Parvana didn't even feel it. Punish her father, would they?

"Stop hitting me!" she yelled.

The Talib was so surprised, he held still for a moment. Parvana saw him pause, and she started to run. She knocked over a pile of turnips at the vegetable stand, and they went rolling all over the street.

Clutching the still-warm nan to her chest, Parvana kept running, her sandals slapping against the pavement. She didn't care if people were staring at her. All she wanted was to get as far away from the soldier as she could, as fast as her legs could carry her.

She was so anxious to get home, she ran right into a woman carrying a child.

"Is that Parvana?"

Parvana tried to get away, but the woman had a firm grip on her arm.

"It is Parvana! What kind of a way is that to carry bread?"

The voice behind the burqa was familiar, but Parvana couldn't remember who it belonged to.

"Speak up, girl! Don't stand there with your mouth open as though you were a fish in the market! Speak up!"

"Mrs. Weera?"

"Oh, that's right, my face is covered. I keep

forgetting. Now, why are you running, and why are you crushing that perfectly good bread?"

Parvana started to cry. "The Taliban...one of the soldiers...he was chasing me."

"Dry your tears. Under such a circumstance, running was a very sensible thing to do. I always thought you had the makings of a sensible girl, and you've just proven me right. Good for you! You've outrun the Taliban. Where are you going with all that bread?"

"Home. I'm almost there."

"We'll go together. I've been meaning to call on your mother for some time. We need a magazine, and your mother is just the person to get it going for us."

"Mother doesn't write any more, and I don't think she'll want company."

"Nonsense. Let's go."

Mrs. Weera had been in the Afghan Women's Union with Mother. She was so sure Mother wouldn't mind her dropping in that Parvana obediently led the way.

"And stop squeezing that bread! It's not going to suddenly jump out of your arms!"

When they were almost at the top step,

Parvana turned to Mrs. Weera. "About Mother. She's not been well."

"Then it's a good thing I'm stopping by to take care of her!"

Parvana gave up. They reached the apartment door and went inside.

Nooria saw only Parvana at first. She took the nan from her. "Is this all you bought? Where's the rice? Where's the tea? How are we supposed to manage with just this?"

"Don't be too hard on her. She was chased out of the market before she could complete her shopping." Mrs. Weera stepped into the room and took off her burqa.

"Mrs. Weera!" Nooria exclaimed. Relief washed over her face. Here was someone who could take charge, who could take some of the responsibility off her shoulders.

Mrs. Weera placed the child she'd been carrying down on the mat beside Ali. The two toddlers eyed each other warily.

Mrs. Weera was a tall woman. Her hair was white, but her body was strong. She had been a physical education teacher before the Taliban made her leave her job.

"What in the world is going on here?" she

asked. In a few quick strides she was in the bathroom, searching out the source of the stench. "Why aren't those diapers washed?"

"We're out of water," Nooria explained. "We've been afraid to go out."

"You're not afraid, are you, Parvana?" She didn't wait for her answer. "Fetch the bucket, girl. Do your bit for the team. Here we go!" Mrs. Weera still talked like she was out on the hockey field, urging everyone to do their best.

"Where's Fatana?" she asked, as Parvana fetched the water bucket. Nooria motioned to the figure on the toshak, buried under a blanket. Mother moaned and tried to huddle down even further.

"She's sleeping," Nooria said.

"How long has she been like this?"

"Four days."

"Where's your father?"

"Arrested."

"Ah, I see." She caught sight of Parvana holding the empty bucket. "Are you waiting for it to rain inside so your bucket will fill itself? Off you go!"

Parvana went.

She made seven trips. Mrs. Weera met her

outside the apartment at the top of the steps and took the first two full buckets from her, emptied them inside and brought back the empty bucket. "We're getting your mother cleaned up, and she doesn't need another pair of eyes on her."

After that, Parvana carried the water inside to the water tank as usual. Mrs. Weera had gotten Mother up and washed. Mother didn't seem to notice Parvana.

She kept hauling water. Her arms were sore, and the blisters on her feet started to bleed again, but she didn't think about that. She fetched water because her family needed it, because her father would have expected her to. Now that Mrs. Weera was there and her mother was up, things were going to get easier, and she would do her part.

Out the door, down the steps, down the street to the tap, then back again, stopping now and then to rest and change carrying arms.

After the seventh trip, Mrs. Weera stopped her.

"You've filled the tank and the wash basin, and there's a full bucket to spare. That's enough for now."

Parvana was dizzy from doing all that exercise with no food and nothing to drink. She wanted some water right away.

"What are you doing?" Nooria asked as Parvana filled a cup from the tank. "You know it has to be boiled first!"

Unboiled water made you sick, but Parvana was so thirsty that she didn't care. She wanted to drink, and raised the cup to her lips.

Nooria snatched it from her hands. "You are the stupidest girl! All we need now is for you to get sick! How could anyone so stupid end up as my sister!"

"That's no way to keep up team spirit," Mrs. Weera said. "Nooria, why don't you get the little ones washed for dinner. Use cold water. We'll let this first batch of boiled water be for drinking."

Parvana went out into the larger room and sat down. Mother was sitting up. She had put on clean clothes. Her hair was brushed and tied back. She looked more like Mother, although she still seemed very tired.

It felt like an eternity before Mrs. Weera handed Parvana a cup of plain boiled water.

"Be careful. It's very hot."

As soon as she could, she drank the water, got another cupful, and drank that, too.

Mrs. Weera and her granddaughter stayed the night. As Parvana drifted off to sleep, she heard her, Nooria and Mother talking quietly together. Mrs. Weera told them about Parvana's brush with the Taliban.

The last thing she heard before she fell asleep was Mrs. Weera saying, "I guess we'll have to think of something else."

SIX

They were going to turn her into a boy.

"As a boy, you'll be able to move in and out of the market, buy what we need, and no one will stop you," Mother said.

"It's a perfect solution," Mrs. Weera said.

"You'll be our cousin from Jalalabad," Nooria said, "come to stay with us while our father is away."

Parvana stared at the three of them. It was as though they were speaking a foreign language, and she didn't have a clue what they were saying.

"If anybody asks about you, we'll say that you have gone to stay with an aunt in Kunduz," Mother said.

"But no one will ask about you."

At these words, Parvana turned her head sharply to glare at her sister. If ever there was a time to say something mean, this was it, but she couldn't think of anything. After all, what Nooria said was true. None of her friends had seen her since the Taliban closed the schools. Her relatives were scattered to different parts of the country, even to different countries. There was no one to ask about her.

"You'll wear Hossain's clothes." Mother's voice caught, and for a moment it seemed as though she would cry, but she got control of herself again. "They will be a bit big for you, but we can make some adjustments if we have to." She glanced over at Mrs. Weera. "Those clothes have been idle long enough. It's time they were put to use."

Parvana guessed Mrs. Weera and her mother had been talking long and hard while she was asleep. She was glad of that. Her mother already looked better. But that didn't mean she was ready to give in.

"It won't work," she said. "I won't look like a boy. I have long hair."

Nooria opened the cupboard door, took out the sewing kit and slowly opened it up. It looked to Parvana as if Nooria was having too much fun as she lifted out the scissors and snapped them open and shut a few times.

"You're not cutting my hair!" Parvana's hands flew up to her head.

"How else will you look like a boy?" Mother asked.

"Cut Nooria's hair! She's the oldest! It's her responsibility to look after me, not my responsibility to look after her!"

"No one would believe me to be a boy," Nooria said calmly, looking down at her body. Nooria being calm just made Parvana madder.

"I'll look like that soon," Parvana said.

"You wish."

"We'll deal with that when the time comes," Mother said quickly, heading off the fight she knew was coming. "Until then, we have no choice. Someone has to be able to go outside, and you are the one most likely to look like a boy."

Parvana thought about it. Her fingers reached up her back to see how long her hair had grown.

"It has to be your decision," Mrs. Weera said. "We can force you to cut off your hair, but you're still the one who has to go outside and act the part. We know this is a big thing we're asking, but I think you can do it. How about it?"

Parvana realized Mrs. Weera was right. They

could hold her down and cut off her hair, but for anything more, they needed her cooperation. In the end, it really was her decision.

Somehow, knowing that made it easier to agree.

"All right," she said. "I'll do it."

"Well done," said Mrs. Weera. "That's the spirit."

Nooria snapped the scissors again. "I'll cut your hair," she said.

"I'll cut it," Mother said, taking the scissors away. "Let's do it now, Parvana. Thinking about it won't make it any easier."

Parvana and her mother went into the washroom where the cement floor would make it easier to clean up the cut-off hair. Mother took Hossain's clothes in with them.

"Do you want to watch?" Mother asked, nodding toward the mirror.

Parvana shook her head, then changed her mind. If this was the last she would see of her hair, then she wanted to see it for as long as she could.

Mother worked quickly. First she cut off a huge chunk in a straight line at her neck. She held it up for Parvana to see.

"I have a lovely piece of ribbon packed away," she said. "We'll tie this up with it, and you can keep it."

Parvana looked at the hair in her mother's hand. While it was on her head, it had seemed important. It didn't seem important any more.

"No, thanks," said Parvana. "Throw it away."

Her mother's lips tightened. "If you're going to sulk about it," she said, and she tossed the hair down to the floor.

As more and more hair fell away, Parvana began to feel like a different person. Her whole face showed. What was left of her hair was short and shaggy. It curled in a soft fringe around her ears. There were no long parts to fall into her eyes, to become tangled on a windy day, to take forever to dry when she got caught in the rain.

Her forehead seemed bigger. Her eyes seemed bigger, too, maybe because she was opening them so wide to be able to see everything. Her ears seemed to stick out from her head.

They look a little funny, Parvana thought, but a nice sort of funny.

I have a nice face, she decided.

Mother rubbed her hands brusquely over Parvana's head to rub away any stray hairs.

"Change your clothes," she said. Then she left the washroom.

All alone, Parvana's hand crept up to the top of her head. Touching her hair gingerly at first, she soon rubbed the palm of her hand all over her head. Her new hair felt both bristly and soft. It tickled the skin on her hand.

I like it, she thought, and she smiled.

She took off her own clothes and put on her brother's. Hossain's shalwar kameez was pale green, both the loose shirt and the baggy trousers. The shirt hung down very low, and the trousers were too long, but by rolling them up at the waist, they were all right.

There was a pocket sewn into the left side of the shirt, near the chest. It was just big enough to hold money and maybe a few candies, if she ever had candies again. There was another pocket on the front. It was nice to have pockets. Her girl clothes didn't have any.

"Parvana, haven't you changed yet?"

Parvana stopped looking at herself in the mirror and joined her family.

The first face she saw was Maryam's. Her little sister looked as if she couldn't quite figure out who had walked into the room.

"It's me, Maryam," Parvana said.

"Parvana!" Maryam laughed as she recognized her.

"Hossain," her mother whispered.

"You look less ugly as a boy than you do as a girl," Nooria said quickly. If Mother started remembering Hossain, she'd just start crying again.

"You look fine," said Mrs. Weera.

"Put this on." Mother handed Parvana a cap. Parvana put it on her head. It was a white cap with beautiful embroidery all over it. Maybe she'd never wear her special red shalwar kameez again, but she had a new cap to take its place.

"Here's some money," her mother said. "Buy what you were not able to buy yesterday." She placed a pakul around Parvana's shoulder. It was her father's. "Hurry back."

Parvana tucked the money into her new pocket. She slipped her feet into her sandals, then reached for her chador.

"You won't be needing that," Nooria said.

Parvana had forgotten. Suddenly she was scared. Everyone would see her face! They would know she wasn't a boy!

She turned around to plead with her mother. "Don't make me do this!"

"You see?" Nooria said in her nastiest voice. "I told you she was too scared."

"It's easy to call someone else scared when you're safe inside your home all the time!" Parvana shot back. She spun around and went outside, slamming the door behind her.

Out on the street, she kept waiting for people to point at her and call her a fake. No one did. No one paid any attention to her at all. The more she was ignored, the more confident she felt.

When she had gone into the market with her father, she had kept silent and covered up her face as much as possible. She had tried her best to be invisible. Now, with her face open to the sunshine, she was invisible in another way. She was just one more boy on the street. She was nothing worth paying attention to.

When she came to the shop that sold tea, rice and other groceries, she hesitated for a slight moment, then walked boldly through the door.

I'm a boy, she kept saying to herself. It gave her courage.

"What do you want?" the grocer asked.

"Some…some tea," Parvana stammered out.

"How much? What kind?" The grocer was gruff, but it was ordinary bad-mood gruff, not gruff out of anger that there was a girl in his shop.

Parvana pointed to the brand of tea they usually had at home. "Is that the cheapest?"

"This one is the cheapest." He showed her another one.

"I'll take the cheapest one. I also need five pounds of rice."

"Don't tell me. You want the cheapest kind. Big spender."

Parvana left the shop with rice and tea, feeling very proud of herself. "I can do this!" she whispered.

Onions were cheap at the vegetable stand. She bought a few.

"Look what I got!" Parvana exclaimed, as she burst through the door of her home. "I did it! I did the shopping, and nobody bothered me."

"Parvana!" Maryam ran to her and gave her

a hug. Parvana hugged her back as best she could with her arms full of groceries.

Mother was back on the toshak, facing the wall, her back to the room. Ali sat beside her, patting her and saying, "Ma-ma-ma," trying to get her attention.

Nooria took the groceries from Parvana and handed her the water bucket.

"As long as you've got your sandals on," she said.

"What's wrong with Mother now?"

"Shhh! Not so loud! Do you want her to hear you? She got upset after seeing you in Hossain's clothes. Can you blame her? Also, Mrs. Weera went home, and that's made her sad. Now, please go and get water."

"I got water yesterday!"

"I had a lot of cleaning to do. Ali was almost out of diapers. Would you rather wash diapers than fetch the water?"

Parvana fetched the water.

"Keep those clothes on," Nooria said when Parvana returned. "I've been thinking about this. If you're going to be a boy outside, you should be a boy inside, too. What if someone comes by?"

That made sense to Parvana. "What about Mother? Won't it upset her to see me in Hossain's clothes all the time?"

"She'll have to get used to it."

For the first time, Parvana noticed the tired lines on Nooria's face. She looked much older than seventeen.

"I'll help you with supper," she offered.

"You? Help? All you'd do is get in my way."

Parvana fumed. It was impossible to be nice to Nooria!

Mother got up for supper and made an effort to be cheerful. She complimented Parvana on her shopping success, but seemed to have a hard time looking at her.

Later that night, when they were all stretched out for sleep, Ali fussed a little.

"Go to sleep, Hossain," Parvana heard her mother say. "Go to sleep, my son."

SEVEN

The next morning, after breakfast, Parvana was back on the street.

"Take your father's writing things and his blanket, and go to the market," Mother told her. "Maybe you can earn some money. You've been watching your father all this time. Just do what he did."

Parvana liked the idea. Yesterday's shopping had gone well. If she could earn money, she might never have to do housework again. The boy disguise had worked once. Why shouldn't it work again?

As she walked to the marketplace, her head felt light without the weight of her hair or chador. She could feel the sun on her face, and a light breeze floating down from the mountain made the air fresh and fine.

Her father's shoulder bag was slung across her chest. It bumped against her legs. Inside were Father's pens and writing paper, and a few items she would try to sell, including her fancy shalwar kameez. Under her arm, Parvana carried the blanket she would sit on.

She chose the same spot where she had gone with her father. It was next to a wall. On the other side of the wall was a house. The wall hid most of it from view. There was a window above the wall, but it had been painted black, in obedience to the Taliban decree.

"If we're at the same place every day, people will get to know we are here, and they will remember us when they need something read or written," Father used to say. Parvana liked that he said "we," as if she was part of his business. The spot was close to home, too. There were busier places in the market, but they took longer to get to, and Parvana wasn't sure she knew the way.

"If anyone asks who you are, say you are Father's nephew Kaseem," Mother said. They had gone over and over the story until Parvana knew it cold. "Say Father is ill, and you have come to stay with the family until he is well again."

It was safer to say Father was ill than to tell people he'd been arrested. No one wanted to look like an enemy of the government.

"Will anyone hire me to read for them?" Parvana asked. "I'm only eleven."

"You still have more education than most people in Afghanistan," Mother said. "However, if they don't hire you, we'll think of something else."

Parvana spread her blanket on the hard clay of the market, arranged her goods for sale to one side, as Father had done, and spread her pens and writing paper out in front of her. Then she sat down and waited for customers.

The first hour went by with no one stopping. Men would walk by, look down at her and keep walking. She wished she had her chador to hide behind. She was certain that at any moment someone would stop, point at her and yell, "Girl!" The word would ring out through the market like a curse, and everyone would stop what they were doing. Staying put that first hour was one of the hardest things she had ever done.

She was looking the other way when someone stopped. She felt the shadow before she saw it, as the man moved between her and the sun. Turning her head, she saw the dark turban that was the uniform of the Taliban. A rifle was slung across his chest as casually as her father's shoulder bag had been slung across hers.

Parvana began to tremble.

"You are a letter reader?" he asked in Pashtu.

Parvana tried to answer, but she couldn't find her voice. Instead, she nodded.

"Speak up, boy! A letter reader who has no voice is no good to me."

Parvana took a deep breath. "I am a letter reader," she said in Pashtu, in a voice that she hoped was loud enough. "I can read and write in Dari and Pashtu." If this was a customer, she hoped her Pashtu would be good enough.

The Talib kept looking down at her. Then he put his hand inside his vest. Keeping his eyes on Parvana, he drew something out of his vest pocket.

Parvana was about to squish her eyes shut and wait to be shot when she saw that the Talib had taken out a letter.

He sat down beside her on the blanket.

"Read this," he said.

Parvana took the envelope from him. The stamp was from Germany. She read the outside.

"This is addressed to Fatima Azima."

"That was my wife," the Talib said.

The letter was very old. Parvana took it out of the envelope and unfolded it. The creases were embedded in the paper.

"Dear Niece," Parvana read. "I am sorry I am not able to be with you at the time of your wedding, but I hope this letter will get to you in time. It is good to be in Germany, away from all the fighting. In my mind, though, I never really leave Afghanistan. My thoughts are always turned to our country, to the family and friends I will probably never see again.

"On this day of your marriage, I send you my very best wishes for your future. Your father, my brother, is a good man, and he will have chosen a good man to be your husband. You may find it hard at first, to be away from your family, but you will have a new family. Soon you will begin to feel you belong there. I hope you will be happy, that you will be blessed with many children, and that you will live to see your son have sons.

"Once you leave Pakistan and return to Afghanistan with your new husband, I will likely lose track of you. Please keep my letter with you, and do not forget me, for I will not forget you.

"Your loving aunt, Sohila."

Parvana stopped reading. The Talib was silent beside her. "Would you like me to read it again?"

He shook his head and held out his hand for the letter. Parvana folded it and gave it back to him. His hands trembled as he put the letter back in the envelope. She saw a tear fall from his eye. It rolled down his cheek until it landed in his beard.

"My wife is dead," he said. "This was among her belongings. I wanted to know what it said." He sat quietly for a few minutes, holding the letter.

"Would you like me to write a reply?" Parvana asked, as she had heard her father do.

The Talib sighed, then shook his head. "How much do I owe you?"

"Pay whatever you like," Parvana said. Her father had also said that.

The Talib took some money out of his pocket and gave it to her. Without another word, he got up off the blanket and went away.

Parvana took a deep breath and let it out

slowly. Up until then, she had seen Talibs only as men who beat women and arrested her father. Could they have feelings of sorrow, like other human beings?

Parvana found it all very confusing. Soon she had another customer, someone who wanted to buy something rather than have something read. All day long, though, her thoughts kept floating back to the Talib who missed his wife.

She had only one other customer before she went home for lunch. A man who had been walking back and forth in front of her blanket finally stopped to talk to her.

"How much do you want for that?" he asked, pointing at her beautiful shalwar kameez.

Mother hadn't told her what price to ask. Parvana tried to remember how her mother used to bargain with vendors in the market when she was able to do the shopping. She would argue the vendor down from whatever price he named first. "They expect you to bargain," she explained, "so they begin with a price so high only a fool would pay it."

Parvana thought quickly. She pictured her aunt in Mazar working hard to do all the embroidery on the dress and around the cuffs of the trousers. She thought of how pretty she'd felt when she wore it, and how much she hated giving it up.

She named a price. The customer shook his head and made a counter-offer, a much lower price. Parvana pointed out the detailed designs of the needlework, then named a price slightly lower than her first one. The customer hesitated, but didn't leave. After a few more prices back and forth, they agreed on an amount.

It was good to make a sale, to have more money to stuff away in the little pocket in the side of her shirt. It felt so good that she almost felt no regret as she watched the vibrant red cloth flutter in the breeze as it was carried away into the crowded labyrinth of the market, never to be seen again.

Parvana stayed on the blanket for another couple of hours, until she realized she had to go to the bathroom. There was nowhere for her to go in the market, so she had to pack up and go home. She went through many of the same motions she went through when she was with her father—packing up the supplies in the shoulder bag, shaking the dust out of the blanket. It made her miss Father.

"Father, come back to us!" she whispered, looking up at the sky. The sun was shining. How could the sun be shining when her father was in jail?

Something caught her eye, a flicker of movement. She thought it came from the blacked-out window, but how could it? Parvana decided she was imagining things. She folded up the blanket and tucked it under her arm. She felt the money she'd earned, tucked safely in her pocket.

Feeling very proud of herself, she ran all the way home.

EIGHT

Mrs. Weera was back. "I'll be moving in this afternoon, Parvana," she said. "You can help me."

Parvana wanted to get back to her blanket, but helping Mrs. Weera would be another change in routine, so that was fine with her. Besides, as long as Mrs. Weera was around, Mother seemed like her old self.

"Mrs. Weera and I are going to work together," Mother announced. "We're going to start a magazine."

"So we'll all have our jobs to do. Nooria will look after the little ones, your mother and I will work on our project, and you will go out to work," Mrs. Weera declared, as though she were assigning positions on the hockey field. "We'll all pull together."

Parvana showed them the money she'd earned.

"Wonderful!" Mother said. "I knew you could do it."

"Father would have made much more," Nooria said, then bit her lip, as if she were attempting to bite back her words.

Parvana was in too good a mood to be bothered.

After tea and nan for lunch, Parvana headed out with Mrs. Weera to get her belongings. Mrs. Weera wore the burqa, of course, but she had such a distinctive way of walking that Parvana was sure she could pick her out of a whole marketplace of women wearing burqas. She walked as though she were rounding up children who were dawdling after class. She walked swiftly, head up and shoulders back. Just to be safe, though, Parvana stayed close to her.

"The Taliban don't usually bother women out alone with small children," Mrs. Weera was saying, "although you can't be certain of that. Fortunately, I can probably outrun any of these soldiers. Outfight them, too, if they tangle with me. I've handled many a teenage boy in my teaching years. There wasn't one I couldn't reduce to tears with a good lecture!"

"I saw a Talib cry this morning," Parvana said, but her words were lost in the whoosh of air as they moved quickly through the streets.

Mrs. Weera had been living with her grandchild in a room even smaller than Parvana's. It was in the basement of a ruined building.

"We are the last of the Weeras," she said. "The bombs took some, the war took others, and pneumonia took the rest."

Parvana didn't know what to say. Mrs. Weera did not sound as though she was looking for sympathy.

"We have the loan of a karachi for the afternoon," Mrs. Weera said. "The owner needs it back this evening to go to work. But we'll manage it all splendidly in one trip, won't we?"

Mrs. Weera had lost a lot of things, too, in bombing raids. "What the bombs didn't get, the bandits did. Makes it easier to move, though, doesn't it?"

Parvana loaded a few quilts and cooking things onto the karachi. Mrs. Weera had everything packed and ready.

"Here's something they didn't get." She took a medal on a bright ribbon out of a box. "I won this in an athletics competition. It means I was the fastest woman runner in all of Afghanistan!"

The sun caught the gleaming gold on the medal. "I have other medals, too," Mrs. Weera said. "Some have been lost, but some I still have." She sighed a little, then caught herself. "Enough recess! Back to work!"

By the end of the afternoon, Mrs. Weera had been moved in and the karachi had been returned. Parvana was too wound up from the day's activities to sit still.

"I'll get some water," she offered.

"You, offering to do something?" Nooria asked. "Are you feeling well?"

Parvana ignored her. "Mother, can I take Maryam to the tap with me?"

"Yes, yes, yes!" Maryam jumped up and down. "I want to go with Parvana!"

Mother hesitated.

"Let her go," Mrs. Weera advised. "Parvana's a boy now. Maryam will be safe."

Mother relented, but first she spoke to Maryam. "What do you call Parvana when you're outside?"

"Kaseem."

"Good. And who is Kaseem?"

"My cousin."

"Very good. Remember that, and do what

Parvana says. Stay right with her, do you promise?"

Maryam promised. She ran to put on her sandals. "They're too tight!" She started to cry.

"She hasn't been outside in over a year," Mother explained to Mrs. Weera. "Of course, her feet have grown."

"Bring them to me and dry your tears," Mrs. Weera told Maryam. The sandals were plastic, all in one piece. "These will do for Ali soon, so I won't cut them. For today, we'll wrap your feet in cloth. Parvana will buy you proper sandals tomorrow. She should be out in the sunshine every day," she said to Mother. "But never mind. Now that I'm here, we'll soon have this family whipped into shape!" She tied several layers of cloth around the child's feet.

"The skin will be tender if she hasn't been outside in such a long time," she told Parvana. "Mind how you go."

"I'm not sure about this," Mother began, but Parvana and her sister hurried out before she could stop them.

Fetching water took a very long time. Maryam had seen nothing but the four walls of their room for almost a year and a half.

Everything outside the door was new to her. Her muscles were not used to the most basic exercise. Parvana had to help her up and down the steps as carefully as she'd had to help Father.

"This is the tap," she said to her sister, as soon as they arrived. Parvana had walked a little ahead, to smooth a pathway free of stones. She turned on the tap so that water gushed out. Maryam laughed. She stuck a hand in the flow, then snatched it back as the cool water touched her skin. She looked at Parvana, eyes wide open. Parvana helped her to do it again. This time, she let the water flow over her.

"Don't swallow any," Parvana warned, then showed her how to splash her face with water. Maryam copied her, getting more water on her clothes than on her face, but at least she had a good time.

One trip was enough for Maryam that first time. The next day, Parvana took Maryam's sandals to the market and used them as a guide to get a bigger pair. She found some used ones that a man was selling along the street. Every day after that, Maryam went to the water tap with Parvana, and bit by bit she started to get stronger.

The days began to fall into a pattern. Parvana went out to the market early every morning, returned home for lunch, then went back to the market in the afternoon.

"I could stay out there if there was a latrine I could use in the market," she said.

"I would want you to come home at mid-day anyway," Mother said. "I want to know that you are all right."

One day, after she had been working for a week, Parvana had an idea. "Mother, I'm seen as a boy, right?"

"That's the idea," Mother said.

"Then I could be your escort," Parvana said. "I could be Nooria's escort, too, and you could both get outside sometimes." Parvana was excited about this. If Nooria got some exercise, maybe she wouldn't be so grumpy. Of course, she wouldn't get much fresh air under the burqa, but at least it would be a change.

"Excellent idea," Mrs. Weera said.

"I don't want you as my escort," Nooria said, but Mother stopped her from saying any more.

"Nooria, Ali should go outside. Parvana is able to manage fine with Maryam, but Ali squirms so much. You will have to hold onto him."

"You should get out sometimes, too, Fatana," Mrs. Weera said to Mother. Mother didn't answer.

For Ali's sake, Nooria went along with the idea. Every day after lunch, Parvana, Nooria, Ali and Maryam went outside for an hour. Ali had been only a few months old when the Taliban came. All he really knew was the little room they had been shut up in for a year and a half. Nooria had not been outside, either, in all that time.

They would walk around the neighborhood until their legs got tired, then they would sit in the sunshine. When there was no one around, Parvana would keep watch, and Nooria would flip up her burqa to let the sun pour down on her face.

"I'd forgotten how good this feels," she said.

When there was no line-up at the water tap, Nooria would wash the little ones right there and save Parvana having to carry that water. Sometimes Mrs. Weera was with them with her grandchild, and all three children were washed at the same time.

Business had good days and bad days. Sometimes Parvana would sit for hours without a customer. She made less money than her father had, but the family was eating, even though most days they ate just nan and tea. The children seemed livelier than they had in a long time. The daily sun and fresh air were doing them a lot of good, although Nooria said they were harder to look after now in the room. They had more energy and always wanted to go outside, which they couldn't do when Parvana was out at work.

At the end of each day, Parvana handed over all the money she'd made. Sometimes Mother asked her to buy nan or something else on the way home. Sometimes, the times Parvana liked best, Mother would come with her to the market to shop for the family— Mrs. Weera's arguments had finally worn her down. Parvana liked having her mother all to herself, even though they didn't talk about anything other than how much cooking oil to buy, or whether they could afford soap that week.

Parvana loved being in the market. She loved watching people move along the streets, loved hearing snatches of conversation that reached her ears, loved reading the letters people brought her.

She still missed her father, but as the weeks went by, she began to get used to him being gone. It helped that she was so busy now. The family didn't talk about him, but she heard Mother and Nooria crying sometimes. Once, Maryam had a nightmare and woke up calling for Father. It took Mother a long time to get her back to sleep.

Then, one afternoon, Parvana saw her father in the market!

He was walking away from her, but Parvana was sure it was him.

"Father!" she called out, springing off her blanket and rushing after him. "Father, I'm here!"

She ran into the crowd, pushing people out of her way, until she finally reached her father and threw her arms around him.

"Father, you're safe! They let you out of prison!"

"Who are you, boy?"

Parvana looked up into a strange face. She backed away.

"I thought you were my father," she said, tears falling down her face.

The man put his hand on her shoulder. "You seem like a fine boy. I'm sorry I am not your father." He paused, then said in a lower voice, "Your father is in prison?" Parvana nodded. "People are released from prison sometimes. Don't give up hope." The man went on his way into the market, and Parvana went back to her blanket.

One afternoon, Parvana was about to shake out her blanket before going home when she noticed a spot of color on the gray wool. She bent down to pick it up.

It was a small square of embroidered cloth, no more than two inches long and an inch wide. Parvana had never seen it before. As she wondered where it had come from, her eyes went up to the blacked-out window where she thought she had seen a flicker of movement a few weeks before. There was no movement now.

The wind must have carried the little piece of embroidery to her blanket, although it hadn't been a very windy day.

She couldn't blame the wind a few days later,

though, when she found a beaded bracelet on her blanket after work. She looked up at the window.

It was open. It swung out over the wall of the house.

Parvana walked closer to get a better look. In the narrow open space, Parvana saw a woman's face. The woman gave Parvana a quick smile, then pulled the window shut.

A few days later, Parvana was sitting watching the tea boys run back and forth between the customers and the tea shop. One of the boys almost collided with a donkey. Parvana was laughing and looking the other way when a tea boy tripped on something near her and spilled a tray of empty tea cups all over her blanket.

The boy sprawled in the dust in front of Parvana. She helped him gather the cups that had rolled away. She handed him the tray and saw his face for the first time. She let out a gasp and slapped a hand across her mouth.

The tea boy was a girl from her class.

NINE

"Shauzia?" Parvana whispered.

"Call me Shafiq. And what do I call you?"

"Kaseem. What are you doing here?"

"The same as you, silly. Look, I have to get back to the tea shop. Will you be here for a while?" Parvana nodded. "Good, I'll come back."

Shauzia picked up her tea things and ran back to the shop. Parvana sat there stunned, watching her old classmate blend in with the other tea boys. It was only by looking at them very carefully that Parvana could distinguish her friend from the others. Then, realizing it wasn't a good idea to stare in case someone asked what she was looking at, Parvana looked away. Shauzia melted back into the market.

Shauzia and Parvana had not been very close in school. They had different friends. Parvana thought Shauzia had been better at spelling, but she couldn't remember for certain.

So there were other girls like her in Kabul! She tried to remember who was in Shauzia's family, but didn't think she knew. Her mind was not on the last two customers of the day, and she was glad when she finally saw Shauzia jogging over to her blanket.

"Where do you live?" Shauzia asked. Parvana pointed. "Let's pack up and walk while we talk. Here, I brought you these." She handed Parvana a small twist of paper holding several dried apricots, something she had not eaten in ages. She counted them. There was one for everyone in her household, and an extra one for her to eat now. She bit into it, and a wonderful sweetness flooded her mouth.

"Thanks!" She put the rest of the apricots in her pocket with the day's wages and began to pack up. There was no little gift left on the blanket today. Parvana didn't mind. Seeing Shauzia was quite enough excitement for one day!

"How long have you been doing this?" Shauzia asked as they walked out of the market.

"Almost a month. How about you?"

"Six months. My brother went to Iran to find work nearly a year ago, and we haven't heard from him since. My father died of a bad heart. So I went to work."

"My father was arrested."

"Have you had any news?"

"No. We went to the prison, but they wouldn't tell us anything. We haven't heard anything at all."

"You probably won't. Most people who are arrested are never heard from again. They just disappear. I have an uncle who disappeared."

Parvana grabbed Shauzia's arm and forced her to stop walking. "My father's coming back," she said. "He is coming back!"

Shauzia nodded. "All right. Your father is different. How's business?"

Parvana let go of Shauzia's arm and started walking again. It was easier to talk about business than about her father. "Some days are good, some days are bad. Do you make much money as a tea boy?"

"Not much. There are a lot of us, so they don't have to pay well. Hey, maybe if we work together, we can come up with a better way to make money."

Parvana thought of the gifts left on the blanket. "I'd like to keep reading letters, at least for part of the day, but maybe there's something we could do for the rest of the day."

"I'd like to sell things off a tray. That way I could move with the crowd. But first I need enough money to buy the tray and the things to sell, and we never have extra money."

"We don't, either. Could we really make a lot of money that way?" Often there was not enough money for kerosene, so they could not light the lamps at night. It made the nights very long.

"From what the other boys tell me, I'd make more than I'm making now, but what's the use of talking about it? Do you miss school?"

The girls talked about their old classmates until they turned down Parvana's street, the one with Mount Parvana at the end of it. It was almost like the old days, when Parvana and her friends would walk home from school together, complaining about teachers and homework assignments.

"I live up here," Parvana said, gesturing up

the flight of stairs on the outside of her building. "You must come up and say hello to everyone."

Shauzia looked at the sky to try to judge how late it was. "Yes, I'll say hello, but after that I'll have to run. When your mother tries to get me to stay for tea, you must back me up and tell her I can't."

Parvana promised, and up the stairs they went.

Everyone was surprised when she walked in with Shauzia! Everyone embraced her as if she was an old friend, even though Parvana didn't think they had ever met before. "I'll let you leave without eating this time," Mother said, "but now that you know where we are, you must bring your whole family by for a meal."

"There's only my mother and me and my two little sisters left," Shauzia said. "My mother doesn't go out. She's sick all the time. We're living with my father's parents and one of his sisters. Everybody fights all the time. I'm lucky to be able to get away from them and go to work."

"Well, you're welcome here any time," Mother said.

"Are you keeping up with your studies?" Mrs. Weera asked.

"My father's parents don't believe in girls being educated, and since we're living in their house, my mother says we have to do what they say."

"Do they mind you dressing like a boy and going out to work?"

Shauzia shrugged. "They eat the food I buy. How could they mind?"

"I've been thinking of starting up a little school here," Mrs. Weera said to Parvana's surprise. "A secret school, for a small number of girls, a few hours a week. You must attend. Parvana will let you know when."

"What about the Taliban?"

"The Taliban will not be invited." Mrs. Weera smiled at her own little joke.

"What will you teach?"

"Field hockey," Parvana replied. "Mrs. Weera was a physical education teacher."

The idea of holding a secret field hockey school in their apartment was so ridiculous that everyone started to laugh. Shauzia was still laughing when she left for home a few minutes later.

There was much to talk about that night at supper.

"We must pay her mother a visit," Mother said. "I'd like to get her story for our magazine."

"How are you going to publish it?" Parvana asked.

Mrs. Weera answered that. "We will smuggle the stories out to Pakistan, where it will be printed. Then we'll smuggle it back in, a few at a time."

"Who will do the smuggling?" Parvana asked, half afraid they were going to make her do it. After all, if they could turn her into a boy, they could have other ideas for her as well.

"Other women in our organization," Mother answered. "We've had visitors while you've been in the market. Some of our members have husbands who support our work and will help us."

Nooria had ideas for the school. She had been planning to go to teacher's college when she finished high school, before the Taliban changed her plans. Father had given her and Parvana lessons for awhile when the schools first closed, but his health was not good, and the practice fell away.

"I could teach arithmetic and history,"

Nooria said. "Mrs. Weera could teach health and science, and Mother could teach reading and writing."

Parvana didn't like the idea of learning from Nooria. As a teacher, she'd be even bossier than she was as a big sister! Still, she couldn't remember the last time she'd seen Nooria excited about something, so she kept quiet.

Almost every day, Parvana and Shauzia would see each other in the market. Parvana waited for her friend to come to her. She was still too shy to run among the pack of tea boys, looking for Shauzia. They talked about some day having enough money to buy trays and things to sell from them, but so far neither could come up with a way to make it happen.

One afternoon, when she was between customers, something landed on Parvana's head. She quickly snatched it off. After checking to make sure no one was watching, she took a look at the latest present from the Window Woman. It was a lovely white handkerchief with red embroidery around the edges.

Parvana was about to look up and smile her thanks at the window, in case the Window

Woman was watching, when Shauzia ran up to the blanket.

"What do you have there?"

Parvana jumped and stuffed the handkerchief in her pocket. "Nothing. How was your day?"

"The usual, but I've got some news. A couple of tea boys heard of a way to make money. Lots of money."

"How?"

"You're not going to like it. Actually, neither do I, but it will pay better than what we've been doing."

"What is it?"

Shauzia told her. Parvana's mouth dropped open.

Shauzia was right. She didn't like it.

TEN

Bones. They were going to dig up bones.

"I'm not sure this is a good idea," Parvana said to Shauzia the next morning. She had her blanket and her father's writing things with her. She hadn't been able to tell her mother about going bone-digging, so she didn't have a reason to leave her usual work things behind.

"I'm glad you brought the blanket. We can use it to haul away the bones." Shauzia ignored Parvana's objections. "Come on. We'd better hurry or we'll get left behind."

Getting left behind did not sound so terrible to Parvana, but with a quick look across the market to the painted-in window with her secret friend, she obediently fell in behind Shauzia as they ran to catch up with the group.

The sky was dark with clouds. They walked for almost an hour, down streets Parvana didn't recognize, until they came to one of the areas of Kabul most heavily destroyed by rockets. There wasn't a single intact building in the whole area, just piles of bricks, dust and rubble.

Bombs had fallen on the cemetery, too. The explosions had shaken up the graves in the ground. Here and there, white bones of the long-dead stuck up out of the rusty-brown earth. Flocks of large black and gray crows cawed and pecked at the ground around the ruined graves of the newer section of the graveyard. The slight breeze carried a rotting stench to where Parvana and Shauzia were standing, on the edge of the cemetery's older section. They watched the boys fan out across the graveyard and start digging.

Parvana noticed a man setting up a large weigh scale next to the partially destroyed wall of a building. "Who's that?"

"That's the bone broker. He buys the bones from us."

"What does he do with them?"

"He sells them to someone else."

"Why would anyone want to buy bones?"

"What do we care, as long as we get paid." Shauzia handed Parvana one of the rough boards she'd brought along to use as a shovel. "Come on, let's get busy."

They walked over to the nearest grave. "What if…what if there's still a body there?" Parvana began. "I mean, what if it's not bones yet?"

"We'll find one with a bone sticking out of it."

They walked around for a moment, looking. It didn't take long.

"Spread out the blanket," Shauzia directed. "We'll pile the bones onto it, then make a bundle out of it."

Parvana spread the blanket, wishing she were back in the market, sitting under the window where her secret friend lived.

The two girls looked at each other, each hoping the other would make the first move.

"We're here to make money, right?" Shauzia said. Parvana nodded. "Then let's make money." She grabbed hold of the bone that was sticking out of the ground and pulled. It came out of the dirt as if it were a carrot being pulled up from a garden. Shauzia tossed it on the blanket.

Not willing to let Shauzia get the better of her, Parvana took up her board and started scraping away the soil. The bombs had done much of the work for them. Many bones were barely covered by dirt and were easy to get at.

"Do you think they'd mind us doing this?" Parvana asked.

"Who?"

"The people who are buried here. Do you think they'd mind us digging them up?"

Shauzia leaned on her board. "Depends on the type of people they were. If they were nasty, stingy people, they wouldn't like it. If they were kind and generous people, they wouldn't mind."

"Would you mind?"

Shauzia looked at her, opened her mouth to speak, then closed it again and returned to her digging. Parvana didn't ask her again.

A few minutes later, Parvana unearthed a skull. "Hey, look at this!" She used the board to loosen the ground around it, then dug the rest of it up with her fingers so she wouldn't break it. She held it up to Shauzia as though it were a trophy.

"It's grinning."

"Of course it's grinning. He's glad to be out in the sunshine after being in the dark ground for so long. Aren't you glad, Mr. Skull?" She made the skull nod. "See? I told you."

"Prop him up on the gravestone. He'll be our mascot."

Parvana placed him carefully on the broken headstone. "He'll be like our boss, watching us to make sure we do it right."

They cleaned out the first grave and moved on to the next, taking Mr. Skull with them. He was joined in a little while by another skull. By the time their blanket was full of bones, there were five skulls perched in a row, grinning down at the girls.

"I have to go to the bathroom," Parvana said. "What am I going to do?"

"I have to go, too." Shauzia looked around. "There's a doorway over there," she said, pointing toward a nearby ruined building. "You go first. I'll keep watch."

"Over me?"

"Over our bones."

"I should go right out here?"

"No one is paying attention to you. It's either that or hold it."

Parvana nodded and put down her board shovel. She'd been holding it for awhile already.

Checking to make sure no one was looking, she headed over to the sheltered doorway.

"Hey, Kaseem."

Parvana looked back at her friend.

"Watch out for land mines," Shauzia said. Then she grinned. Parvana grinned back. Shauzia was probably joking, but she kept her eyes open anyway.

"Kabul has more land mines than flowers," her father used to say. "Land mines are as common as rocks and can blow you up without warning. Remember your brother."

Parvana remembered the time someone from the United Nations had come to her class with a chart showing the different kinds of land mines. She tried to remember what they looked like. All she could remember was that some were disguised as toys—special mines to blow up children.

Parvana peered into the darkness of the doorway. Sometimes armies would plant mines in buildings as they left an area. Could someone have planted a land mine there? Would she blow up if she stepped inside?

She knew she was faced with three choices. One choice was to not go to the bathroom until she got home. That was not possible—she really couldn't hold it much longer. Another choice was to go to the bathroom outside the doorway, where people might see her and figure out she was a girl. The third was to step into the darkness, go to the bathroom in private, and hope she didn't explode.

She picked the third choice. Taking a deep breath and uttering a quick prayer, she stepped through the doorway. She did not explode.

"No land mines?" Shauzia asked when Parvana returned.

"I kicked them out of the way," Parvana joked, but she was still shaking.

When Shauzia came back from her trip to the doorway, they made a bundle of the bones in the blanket, with the skulls thrown in, and carried it together over to the bone broker and his scales. He had to fill the bucket on the scales three times to accommodate all their bones. He added up the weight, named an amount, and counted up the money.

Parvana and Shauzia didn't say anything until they were well away from the bone broker's stall. They were afraid he might have made a mistake and given them too much.

"This is as much as I made in three days last week," Parvana said.

"I told you we'd make money!" Shauzia said as she handed half the cash to Parvana. "Shall we quit for the day or keep digging?"

"Keep digging, of course." Mother expected her for lunch, but she'd think of something to tell her.

In the middle of the afternoon, there was a small break in the clouds. A stream of bright sunlight hit the graveyard.

Parvana gave Shauzia a nudge, and they looked out over the mounds of dug-up graves, at the boys, sweaty and smudged with dirt, at the piles of bones beside them, gleaming white in the sudden sunshine.

"We have to remember this," Parvana said. "When things get better and we grow up, we have to remember that there was a day when we were kids when we stood in a graveyard and dug up bones to sell so that our families could eat."

"Will anyone believe us?"

"No. But we will know it happened."

"When we're rich old ladies, we'll drink tea together and talk about this day."

The girls leaned on their board shovels, watching the other children work. Then the sun went back in, and they got back to work themselves. They filled their blanket again before stopping for the day.

"If we turn all this money over to our families, they'll find things to spend it on, and we'll never get our trays," Shauzia said. "I think we should keep something back, not turn it all over to them."

"Are you going to tell your family what you were doing today?"

"No," Shauzia said.

"Neither will I," Parvana said. "I'm just going to turn over my regular amount, maybe a little bit more. I'll tell them some day, but not just now."

They parted, arranging to meet again early the next morning for another day of bone digging.

Before going home, Parvana went to the water tap. Her clothes were dirty. She washed them off as best she could while they were still on her. She took the money out of her pocket and divided it in two. Some she put back in her pocket to give to her mother. The rest she hid in the bottom of her shoulder bag, next to her father's writing paper.

Finally, she stuck her whole head under the tap, hoping the cold water would wash the images of what she had done all day out of her head. But every time she closed her eyes, she saw Mr. Skull and his companions lined up on the gravestones, grinning at her.

ELEVEN

"You're all wet," Maryam said as soon as Parvana walked through the door.

"Are you all right?" Mother rushed up to her. "Where were you? Why didn't you come home for lunch?"

"I was working," Parvana said. She tried to twist away, but her mother held her firmly by the shoulders.

"Where were you?" Mother repeated. "We've been sitting here terrified that you had been arrested!"

All that she had seen and done that day came rushing into Parvana's mind. She threw her arms around her mother's neck and cried. Mother held her until she was calm again and could talk.

"Now, tell me where you were today."

Parvana found she could not bear to say it to her mother's face, so she pressed herself up against the wall and told her.

"I was digging up graves."

"You were doing what?" Nooria asked.

Parvana left the wall and sat down on the toshak. She told them all about her day.

"Did you see real bones?" Maryam asked. Mrs. Weera told her to hush.

"So this is what we've become in Afghanistan," Mother said. "We dig up the bones of our ancestors in order to feed our families!"

"Bones are used for all sorts of things," Mrs. Weera replied. "Chicken feed, cooking oil, soap and buttons. I've heard of animal bones being used this way, not human bones."

"Was it worth it?" Nooria asked. "How much money did you make?"

Parvana took the money out of her pocket, then dug the rest of the money out of the shoulder bag. She put it all on the floor for everyone to see.

"All that for digging up graves," Mrs. Weera breathed.

"Tomorrow you'll go back to reading letters. No more of this digging!" Mother declared. "We don't need money that badly!"

"No," Parvana said to her mother.

"I beg your pardon?"

"I don't want to quit yet. Shauzia and I want to buy trays, and things to sell from the trays. I can follow the crowd that way, instead of waiting for the crowd to come to me. I can make more money."

"We are managing fine on what you earn reading letters."

"No, Mother, we're not," Nooria said.

Mother spun around to scold Nooria for talking back, but Nooria kept talking. "We have nothing left to sell. What Parvana earns keeps us in nan, rice and tea, but there's nothing extra. We need money for rent, for propane, for fuel for the lamps. If she can make money this way, and she's willing to do it, then I think she should be allowed."

It was Parvana's turn to be stunned. Nooria taking her side? Such a thing had never happened before.

"I'm glad your father isn't here to hear you talk to me with such disrespect!"

"That's just it," Mrs. Weera said gently. "Their father isn't here. These are unusual times. They call for ordinary people to do unusual things, just to get by."

In the end, Mother relented. "You must tell me everything that happens," she told Parvana. "We will put it in the magazine, so that everyone will know."

From then on, she sent Parvana off to work with a little packet of nan for her lunch, "since you won't be back at mid-day." Although Parvana got very hungry during the day, she couldn't bear to eat in the middle of the field of bones. She gave her nan to one of Kabul's many beggars, so that someone would get some use out of it.

At the end of two weeks, they had enough money to buy the trays, with straps to go around their necks to carry them.

"We should sell things that don't weigh much," Shauzia said. They decided on cigarettes, which they could buy in big cartons and sell by the pack. They also sold chewing gum, by the pack and sometimes by the stick. Boxes of matches filled up the empty spaces on the trays.

"My tea boy days are over!" Shauzia said gleefully.

"I'm just happy to be out of the graveyard," Parvana said. She was learning to walk and balance the tray at the same time. She didn't want all her lovely goods to fall into the dirt.

The first morning back at her letter-reading post was almost over before she felt something drop on her head again.

Her aim is getting good, Parvana thought. Two direct hits in a row.

This time, the gift was a single red wooden bead. Parvana rolled it around her fingers and wondered about the woman who had sent it.

Her graveyard stint over, she was back to going outside with Nooria and the little ones in the middle of the day. A change had come over Nooria. She hadn't said anything nasty to Parvana in ages.

Or maybe it's me who's changed, Parvana thought. Arguing with Nooria simply didn't make sense any more.

In the afternoon, she would meet up with Shauzia, and the two of them would wander around Kabul looking for customers. They did not earn as much as they did in the graveyard, but they did all right. Parvana was getting to know Kabul.

"There's a crowd," Shauzia said one Friday afternoon, pointing at the sports stadium.

Thousands of people were headed into the stands.

"Wonderful!" exclaimed Parvana. "People will want to smoke and chew gum while they watch a soccer game. We'll sell out. Let's go!"

They ran over to the stadium entrance as fast as they could without bouncing their cigarettes onto the ground. Several Taliban soldiers were urging people inside, yelling at them to hurry. They pushed and shoved people through the stadium gates, swinging their sticks to get the slow ones to move faster.

"Let's avoid those guys," Shauzia suggested. She and Parvana dodged around some groups of men and slipped into the stadium.

The stadium stands were almost full. The two girls were a little intimidated by so many people and stayed next to each other as they went up into the bleachers to sell their wares.

"It's awfully quiet for a soccer game," Shauzia said.

"The game hasn't started yet. Maybe the cheering will start when the players come on the field." Parvana had seen sports events on television, and people in the stands always cheered.

No one was cheering. The men did not look at all happy to be there.

"This is very strange," Parvana whispered into Shauzia's ear.

"Look out!" A large group of Taliban soldiers walked onto the field close to them. The girls ducked down low so they could see the field but the Taliban couldn't see them.

"Let's get out of here," Shauzia said. "No one's buying anything from us, and I don't know why, but I'm getting scared."

"As soon as the game starts, we'll go," Parvana said. "If we try to leave now, people will look at us."

More men moved onto the field, but they weren't soccer players. Several men were brought in with their hands tied behind their backs. A heavy-looking table was carried out by two of the soldiers.

"I think those men are prisoners," Shauzia whispered.

"What are prisoners doing at a soccer game?" Parvana whispered back. Shauzia shrugged.

One of the men was untied, then bent over the table. Several soldiers held him down, his arms stretched out across the table-top.

Parvana didn't have a clue what was going on. Where were the soccer players?

All of a sudden one of the soldiers took out a sword, raised it above his head and brought it down on the man's arm. Blood flew in every direction. The man cried out in pain.

Next to Parvana, Shauzia started screaming. Parvana clamped her hand over Shauzia's mouth and pulled her down to the floor of the stadium stands. The rest of the stadium was quiet. There was still no cheering.

"Keep your heads down, boys," a kind voice above Parvana said. "There will be time enough when you are old to see such things."

The cigarettes and gum had fallen off their trays, but the men around them gathered up the spilled items and returned them to the girls.

Parvana and Shauzia stayed huddled among people's feet, listening to the sword thwack down on six more arms.

"These men are thieves," the soldiers called out to the crowd. "See how we punish thieves? We cut off one of their hands! See what we do!"

Parvana and Shauzia did not look. They kept

their heads down until the man with the kind voice said, "It's over for another week. Come, now, raise yourselves up." He and several other men surrounded Parvana and Shauzia, escorting them out of the stadium.

Just before she left, Parvana caught a glimpse of a young Talib man, too young to have a beard.

He was holding up a rope strung with four severed hands, like beads on a necklace. He was laughing and showing off his booty to the crowd. Parvana hoped Shauzia hadn't seen.

"Go home, boys," the kind man told them. "Go home and remember better things."

TWELVE

Parvana stayed home for a few days. She went out to get water, and she and Nooria took the little ones out into the sunshine, but beyond that, she wanted to be with her family.

"I need a break," she told her mother. "I don't want to see anything ugly for a little while."

Mother and Mrs. Weera had heard about the events at the stadium from other women's group members. Some had husbands or brothers who had been there. "This goes on every Friday," Mother said. "What century are we living in?"

"Will Father be taken there?" Parvana wanted to ask, but she didn't. Her mother wouldn't know.

During her days at home, Parvana coached Maryam on her counting, tried to learn mending from Nooria and listened to Mrs. Weera's stories. They weren't as good as her father's stories. Mostly they were descriptions of field hockey games or other athletic events. Still, they were entertaining, and Mrs. Weera was so enthusiastic about them that she made other people enthusiastic, too.

No one said anything to Parvana when the bread ran out, but she got up and went to work that day anyway. Some things just had to be taken care of.

"I'm glad you're back," Shauzia said when she saw Parvana in the market. "I missed you. Where were you?"

"I didn't feel like working," Parvana replied. "I wanted some quiet days."

"I wouldn't mind some of those, but it's noisier in my home than it is out here."

"Is your family still arguing?"

Shauzia nodded. "My father's parents never really liked my mother anyway. Now they depend on her. It makes them grumpy. Mother's grumpy because we have to live with them since there's no place else to go. So every-body is grumpy. If they're not actually arguing, they sit and glare at each other."

Parvana thought about how it felt in her home sometimes, with everyone going around with tight lips and unshed tears in their eyes. It sounded even worse in Shauzia's house.

"Can I tell you a secret?" Shauzia asked. She led Parvana over to a low wall, and they sat down.

"Of course you can tell me. I won't tell anybody."

"I'm saving money, a little bit each day. I'm getting out of here."

"Where? When?"

Shauzia kicked at the wall in a rhythm, but Parvana stopped her. She'd seen the Taliban hit a child for banging on an old board like it was a drum. The Taliban hated music.

"I'll stay until next spring," Shauzia said. "I'll have a lot of money saved by then, and it's better not to travel in the winter."

"Do you think we'll still have to be boys in the spring? That's a long time from now."

"I want to still be a boy then," Shauzia insisted. "If I turn back into a girl, I'll be stuck at home. I couldn't stand that."

"Where will you go?"

"France. I'll get on a boat and go to France."

"Why France?" she asked.

Shauzia's face brightened. "In every picture

I've seen of France, the sun is shining, people are smiling, and flowers are blooming. France people must have bad days, too, but I don't think their bad days can be very bad, not bad like here. In one picture I saw a whole field of purple flowers. That's where I want to go. I want to walk into that field and sit down in the middle of it, and not think about anything."

Parvana struggled to remember her map of the world. "I'm not sure you can get to France by boat."

"Sure I can. I've got it all figured out. I'll tell a group of nomads that I'm an orphan, and I'll travel with them into Pakistan. My father told me they go back and forth with the seasons, looking for grass for their sheep. In Pakistan, I head down to the Arabian Sea, get on a boat, and go to France!" She spoke as if nothing could be more simple. "The first boat I get on might not go directly to France, but at least I'll get away from here. Everything will be easy once I get away from here."

"You'll go by yourself!" Parvana couldn't imagine undertaking such a journey on her own.

"Who will notice one little orphan boy?"

Shauzia replied. "No one will pay any attention to me. I just hope I haven't left it too late."

"What do you mean?"

"I'm starting to grow." Her voice dropped almost to a whisper. "My shape is changing. If it changes too much, I'll turn back into a girl, and then I'll be stuck here. You don't think I'll grow too fast, do you? Maybe I should leave before the spring. I don't want things to pop out of me all of a sudden."

Parvana did not want Shauzia to leave, but she tried to be honest with her friend. "I can't remember how it happened with Nooria. Mostly, I watched her hair grow. But I don't think growing happens all of a sudden. I'd say you have time."

Shauzia started to kick the building again. Then she stood up so she wouldn't be tempted. "That's what I'm counting on."

"You'll leave your family? How will they eat?"

"I can't help that!" Shauzia's voice rose and caught, as she tried not to cry. "I just have to get out of here. I know that makes me a bad person, but what else can I do? I'll die if I have to stay here!"

Parvana remembered arguments between her

father and mother—her mother insisting they leave Afghanistan, her father insisting they stay. For the first time, Parvana wondered why her mother didn't just leave. In an instant, she answered her own question. She couldn't sneak away with four children to take care of.

"I just want to be an ordinary kid again," Parvana said. "I want to sit in a classroom and go home and eat food that someone else has worked for. I want my father to be around. I just want a normal, boring life."

"I don't think I could ever sit in a classroom again," Shauzia said. "Not after all this." She adjusted her tray of cigarettes. "You'll keep my secret?"

Parvana nodded.

"Do you want to come with me?" Shauzia asked. "We could look after each other."

"I don't know." She could leave Afghanistan, but could she leave her family? She didn't think so.

"I have a secret, too," she said. She reached into her pocket and pulled out the little gifts she'd received from the woman at the window. She told Shauzia where they had come from.

"Wow," Shauzia said. "That's a real mystery.

I wonder who she could be. Maybe she's a princess!"

"Maybe we can save her!" Parvana said. She saw herself climbing up the wall, smashing the painted-over window with her bare fist and helping the princess down to the ground. The princess would be wearing silk and jewels. Parvana would swing her up onto the back of a fast horse, and they'd ride through Kabul in a cloud of dust.

"I'll need a fast horse," she said.

"How about one of those?" Shauzia pointed to a herd of long-haired sheep snuffling through the garbage on the ground of the market.

Parvana laughed, and the girls went back to work.

At her mother's suggestion, Parvana had bought a few pounds of dried fruit and nuts. Nooria and Maryam put them into smaller bags, enough for a snack for one person. Parvana sold these from her blanket and her tray.

In the afternoon, she and Shauzia wandered around the market looking for customers. Sometimes they went to the bus depot, but they had a lot of competition there. Many boys were trying to sell things. They would run right up to someone and stand in the person's way, saying, "Buy my gum! Buy my fruit! Buy my cigarettes!" Parvana and Shauzia were too shy for that. They preferred to wait for customers to notice them.

Parvana was tired. She wanted to sit in a classroom and be bored by a geography lesson. She wanted to be with her friends and talk about homework and games and what to do on school holidays. She didn't want to know any more about death or blood or pain.

The marketplace ceased to be interesting. She no longer laughed when a man got into an argument with a stubborn donkey. She was no longer interested in the snippets of conversation she heard from people strolling by. Everywhere, there were people who were hungry and sick. Women in burqas sat on the pavement and begged, their babies stretched across their laps.

And there was no end to it. This wasn't a summer vacation that would end and then life would get back to normal. This was normal, and Parvana was tired of it.

Summer had come to Kabul. Flowers pushed up out of the ground, not caring about the Taliban or land mines, and actually bloomed, just as they did in peace time.

Parvana's home, with its little window, grew very hot during the long June days, and the little ones were cranky at night with the heat. Even Maryam lost her good humor and whined along with the two youngest children. Parvana was glad to be able to leave in the morning.

Summer brought fruit into Kabul from the fertile valleys—those that had not been bombed into extinction. Parvana brought treats home for her family on the days she made a bit more money. They had peaches one week, plums the next.

The clear mountain passes brought traders from all over Afghanistan into Kabul. From her blanket in the marketplace, and when she walked around selling cigarettes with Shauzia, Parvana saw tribal peoples from Bamiyan, from the Registan Desert region near Kandahar, and from the Wakhan Corridor near China.

Sometimes these men would stop and buy dried fruit or cigarettes from her. Sometimes they had something for her to read or write. She would always ask where they were from and what it was like there, so she could have something new to tell her family when she went home. Sometimes they told her about the weather. Sometimes they told of the beautiful mountains or the fields of opium poppies blooming into flower, or the orchards heavy with fruit. Sometimes they told her of the war, of battles they had seen and people they had lost. Parvana remembered it all to tell her family when she got home.

Through Mother's and Mrs. Weera's women's group, a secret little school was started. Nooria was the teacher. The Taliban would close down any school they discovered, so Nooria and Mrs. Weera were very careful. This school held only five girls, including Maryam. They were all around her age. They were taught in two different groups, never at the same time two days running. Sometimes the students came to Nooria, sometimes Nooria went to the students. Sometimes Parvana was her escort. Sometimes she carried a squirming Ali.

"He's getting too big to be carried around,"

Nooria said to Parvana on one of their noon-day walks. Mother had allowed Nooria to leave Ali at home, to get a break from him. They only had Maryam with them, and she was no trouble.

"How are your students doing?"

"They can't learn much in a few hours a week," Nooria replied. "And we don't have any books or school supplies. Still, I guess it's better than nothing."

The little gifts from the window kept landing on Parvana's blanket every couple of weeks. Sometimes it was a piece of embroidery. Sometimes it was a piece of candy or a single bead.

It was as if the Window Woman was saying, "I'm still here," in the only way she could. Parvana checked carefully around her blanket every time she went to leave the market, in case one of the gifts had rolled off.

One afternoon, she heard sounds coming from above her. A man was very angry. He was shouting at a woman who was crying and screaming. Parvana heard thuds and more screams. Without thinking, she sprang to her feet and looked up at the window, but she couldn't see anything through the painted glass.

"What goes on in a man's house is his own business," a voice behind her said. She spun around to see a man holding out an envelope. "Forget about that and turn your mind to your own business. I have a letter for you to read."

She was planning to tell her family about the whole incident that night, but she didn't get the chance. Instead, her family had something to tell her.

"You'll never guess," her mother said. "Nooria's getting married."

THIRTEEN

"But you've never even met him!" Parvana exclaimed to Nooria the next day at noon. It was the first chance they'd had to talk about it, just the two of them.

"Of course I've met him. His family and ours were neighbors for many years."

"But that was when he was a boy. I thought you wanted to go back to school!"

"I will be going back to school," Nooria said. "Didn't you listen to anything Mother was saying last night? I'll be living in Mazar-e-Sharif, in the north. The Taliban aren't in that part of Afghanistan. Girls can still go to school there. Both of his parents are educated. I can finish school, and they'll even send me to the university in Mazar."

All of this was written in a letter that had arrived while Parvana was out at work. The women in the groom's family belonged to the same women's group as Mother. The letter had passed from one member of the group to another until it finally reached Mother. Parvana had read the letter, but she still had a lot of questions.

"Do you really want to do this?"

Nooria nodded. "Look at my life here, Parvana. I hate living under the Taliban. I'm tired of looking after the little ones. My school classes happen so seldom, they're of almost no value. There's no future for me here. At least in Mazar I can go to school, walk the streets without having to wear a burqa, and get a job when I've completed school. Maybe in Mazar I can have some kind of life. Yes, I want to do this."

There was a lot of discussion in the following few days about what would happen next. Parvana, out at work, had no voice in these discussions. She was merely informed of the plans when she got home in the evening.

"We'll go to Mazar for the wedding," Mother announced. "We can all stay with your aunt while the wedding is prepared. Then Nooria will go to live with her new family. We will return to Kabul in October."

"We can't leave Kabul!" Parvana exclaimed. "What about Father? What will happen if he gets out of prison and we're not here? He won't know where to look for us!"

"I'll be here," Mrs. Weera said. "I can tell your father where you are and look after him until you get back."

"I'm not sending Nooria off to Mazar all by herself," Mother said. "And since you are a child, you will come with us."

"I'm not going," Parvana insisted. She even stamped her feet.

"You will do as you're told," Mother said. "All this running around wild in the streets has made you think you're above yourself."

"I'm not going to Mazar!" Parvana repeated, stamping her feet again.

"Since your feet want to move around so much, you'd better take them out for a walk," Mrs. Weera said. "You can fetch some water while you're at it."

Parvana grabbed the bucket and got some satisfaction out of slamming the door behind her. ·

Parvana glowered for three days. Finally, Mother said, "You can take that awful frown off your face. We've decided to leave you here. Not because of your bad behavior. A child of eleven has no business telling her mother what she will and will not do. We're leaving you here because it will be too difficult to explain your appearance. Your aunt will keep your secret, of course, but we can't count on everyone to be so careful. We can't take the chance of word about you getting back here."

Although she was glad to remain in Kabul, Parvana found herself sulking that they weren't taking her with them. "I'm not satisfied with anything any more," she told Shauzia the next day.

"Neither am I," Shauzia said. "I used to think that if only I could sell things from a tray, I'd be happy, but I'm not happy at all. I make more money this way than I did as a tea boy, but it's not enough to make any real difference. We still go hungry. My family still argues all the time. Nothing is better."

"What's the answer?"

"Maybe someone should drop a big bomb on the country and start again."

"They've tried that," Parvana said. "It only made things worse."

One of the women in the local branch of the women's group was going to accompany

Parvana's family to the city of Mazar. Her husband would go with them as the official escort. If the Taliban asked, Mother would be the husband's sister, and Nooria, Maryam and Ali would be the nieces and nephews.

Nooria cleaned out the family cupboard one last time. Parvana watched her pack up her things. "If all goes well, we'll be in Mazar in a couple of days," Nooria said.

"Are you scared?" Parvana asked. "It's a long journey."

"I keep thinking of things that can go wrong, but Mother says everything will be fine." They would be traveling together in the back of a truck. "As soon as I get out of Taliban territory, I'm going to throw off my burqa and tear it into a million pieces."

Parvana went to the market the next day to buy the family some food for the journey. She wanted to buy Nooria a present, too. She wandered through the market looking at things for sale. She finally decided on a pen in a beaded case. Every time Nooria used it at university, and later when she became a real school teacher, she would think of Parvana.

"We'll be gone for most of the summer,"

Mother reminded Parvana the night before they left. "You'll be fine with Mrs. Weera. Do what she tells you, and don't give her any trouble."

"Parvana and I will be good company for each other," Mrs. Weera said, "and by the time you get back, the magazine should be coming in from Pakistan, all printed and ready to distribute."

They left very early the next day. The mid-July morning was fresh but held the promise of hot weather to follow.

"We'd best be going," Mother said. Since there was no one else on the street, Mother, Nooria and Mrs. Weera had their burqas flipped up so their faces could be seen.

Parvana kissed Ali, who squirmed and fussed, grumpy from being woken up early. Mother got him settled on the floor of the truck. Parvana said goodbye to Maryam after that, then lifted her into the truck.

"We will see you by the middle of September," Mother said as she hugged Parvana. "Make me proud of you."

"I will," Parvana said, trying not to cry.

"I don't know when we'll see each other

again," Nooria said just before she climbed into the truck. She had Parvana's gift clutched in her hand.

"It won't be long," Parvana said, grinning even though tears fell from her eyes. "As soon as your new husband realizes how bossy you are, he'll send you back to Kabul as fast as he can."

Nooria laughed and climbed into the truck. She and Mother covered themselves with their burqas. The women's group member and her husband were sitting in the front seat. Parvana and Mrs. Weera watched and waved as the truck drove out of sight.

"I think we could both use a cup of tea," Mrs. Weera said, and they went upstairs.

Parvana found the next few weeks to be a strange time. With only herself, Mrs. Weera and Mrs. Weera's grandchild, the apartment seemed almost empty. Fewer people meant fewer chores, less noise and more free time. Parvana even missed Ali's fussing. As the weeks went by, she looked forward more and more to everyone coming back.

Still, she did enjoy having more free time. For the first time since Father's arrest, she took his books out of their secret place in the cupboard. Evenings were spent reading and listening to Mrs. Weera's stories.

Mrs. Weera believed in trusting her. "In some parts of the country, girls your age are getting married and having babies," she said. "I'm here if you need me, but if you want to be responsible for yourself, that's fine, too."

She insisted that Parvana keep some of her wages as pocket money. Sometimes Parvana would treat Shauzia to lunch at one of the kebab stands in the market. They'd find a sheltered place to go to the bathroom and keep working all day. Parvana preferred to come home at the end of the day, rather than at noon. It meant that one more day was over, and her family would soon be home.

Toward the end of August, there was a bad rainstorm. Shauzia had already gone home. She had seen the darkening sky and didn't feel like getting wet.

Parvana wasn't so clever, and she got caught in the rain. She covered her tray with her arms to keep her cigarettes dry and ducked into a bombed-out building. She would wait out the storm there and go home when it was over.

The darkness outside made the inside even blacker. It took awhile for her eyes to adjust. While she waited for that to happen, she leaned against the doorway, watching the rain turn Kabul's dust into mud.

Gusts of wind mixed with driving rain forced Parvana deeper inside the building. Hoping there were no land mines, she found a dry spot and sat down. The pounding of the rain beat a steady rhythm as it hit the ground. Parvana began to nod. In a little while, she was asleep.

When she woke up, the rain had stopped, although the sky was no lighter.

"It must be late," Parvana said out loud.

It was then that she heard the sound of a woman crying.

FOURTEEN

The sound was too soft and too sad to be startling.

"Hello?" Parvana called out, not too loudly.

It was too dark to see where the woman was sitting. Parvana rummaged around on her tray until she found a box of the matches she sold with the cigarettes. She struck one, and the light flared up. She held the flame out in front of her, looking for the crying woman.

It took three matches before she saw the figure huddled against the nearby wall. She kept striking matches so she could see as she made her way over to the woman.

"What's your name?" Parvana asked. The woman kept crying. "I'll tell you my name, then. It's Parvana. I should tell you that my name is Kaseem, because I'm pretending to be a boy. I'm dressed like a boy so that I can earn some money, but I'm really a girl. So now you know my secret."

The woman said nothing. Parvana glanced out the door. It was getting late. If she was going to be home before curfew, she'd have to leave now.

"Come with me," Parvana said. "My mother is away, but Mrs. Weera is at home. She can fix any problem." She struck another match and held it up to the woman's face. It suddenly dawned on her that she could see the woman's face. It wasn't covered up.

"Where is your burqa?" She looked around but couldn't see one. "Are you outside without a burqa?"

The woman nodded.

"What are you doing outside without a burqa? You could get in a lot of trouble for that."

The woman just shook her head.

Parvana had an idea. "Here's what we'll do. I'll go home and borrow Mrs. Weera's burqa and bring it back to you. Then we'll go back to my place together. All right?"

Parvana started to stand up, but the woman grabbed onto her arm.

Again Parvana looked out the door at the coming night. "I have to let Mrs. Weera know where I am. She's fine with me being out during the day, but if I'm not back at night, she'll be worried." Still the woman did not let go.

Parvana didn't know what to do. She couldn't stay in the building all night, but this frightened woman clearly did not want to be left alone. Groping in the dark for her tray, she found two little bags of dried fruit and nuts.

"Here," she said, handing one to the woman. "We'll think better if we eat."

The woman downed the fruit and nuts in almost one swallow. "You must be starving," Parvana said, passing her another bag.

Parvana chewed and thought and finally decided what to do. "This is the best suggestion I have," she said. "If you have a better idea, let me know. Otherwise, this is what we'll do. We'll wait until it gets very, very dark. Then we'll head back to my place together. Do you have a chador?"

The woman shook her head. Parvana wished she had her pakul, but it was summer, so she had left it at home.

"Do you agree?" Parvana asked.

The woman nodded.

"Good. I think we should move close to the

door. That way, when it's time, we can see our way out to the street without lighting a match. I don't want to draw any attention to us."

With a bit of gentle pulling, Parvana got the woman to her feet. Carefully they made their way to a spot just inside the door, but still hidden from the view of anyone passing by. They waited in silence for night to fall.

Kabul was a dark city at night. It had been under curfew for more than twenty years. Many of the street lights had been knocked out by bombs, and many of those still standing did not work.

"Kabul was the hot spot of central Asia," Parvana's mother and father used to say. "We used to walk down the streets at midnight, eating ice cream. Earlier in the evening, we would browse through book shops and record stores. It was a city of lights, progress and excitement."

Parvana could not even imagine what it had looked like then.

Before long it was as dark as it would get. "Stay right with me," Parvana said, although she needn't have bothered. The woman was gripping her hand tightly. "It's not far, but I don't know how long it will take us tonight. Don't worry." She smiled, pretending to be brave. She knew it was too dark in the doorway for the woman to see her smile, but it made Parvana feel better.

"I'm Malali, leading the troops through enemy territory," she murmured to herself. That helped, too, although it was hard to feel like a battle heroine with a cigarette tray hanging around her neck.

The narrow, winding streets of the marketplace were very different in the dark. Parvana could hear their footsteps echo along the narrow corridors. She was about to tell the woman to walk more softly, that the Taliban had made it a crime for women to make noise when they walked, but she changed her mind. If the Taliban caught them out after curfew and with the woman without a burqa or a head covering at all, the noise they were making would be the least of their problems. Parvana remembered the scene in the stadium. She didn't want to know what the Taliban would do to her and her companion.

Parvana saw headlights approaching and pulled the woman into another doorway until the truck filled with soldiers moved on down the street. Several times they almost tripped on the uneven pavement. For one long, heart-stopping minute, Parvana thought she was lost. Finally she got her bearings, and they kept moving.

When they got to Parvana's street, she started to run, and she pulled the woman along with her. She was so scared by this point, she thought if she didn't get home right away, she would collapse.

"You're back!" Mrs. Weera was so relieved, she hugged both Parvana and the woman before she realized what she was doing. "You've brought someone with you! You are very welcome here, my dear." She took a critical look at the woman. "Parvana, you didn't bring her through the streets like that? With no burqa?"

Parvana explained what had happened. "I think she's in trouble," she said.

Mrs. Weera didn't hesitate. She put her arm around the woman. "We'll get the details later. There's warm water for you to wash in, and hot food for supper. You don't look much older than Parvana!"

Parvana took a good look at her companion. She hadn't seen the woman in the light before. She looked a little bit younger than Nooria.

"Fetch me some clean clothes," Mrs. Weera told Parvana. Parvana took a shalwar kameez of Mother's out of the cupboard, and Mrs. Weera took the young woman into the wash-room and closed the door.

Parvana restocked her tray for the next day, then spread the meal cloth out on the floor. By the time she had put out the nan and the cups for tea, Mrs. Weera emerged from the wash-room with their guest.

Dressed in Mother's clean clothes, her hair washed and pulled back, the woman looked less scared and more tired. She managed to drink half a cup of tea and eat a few mouthfuls of rice before she fell asleep.

She was still sleeping when Parvana left for work the next morning.

"Fetch me some water, please, dear," Mrs. Weera asked before Parvana went off to the market. "That poor girl's clothes need washing."

Finally, that night, after eating supper, the girl was able to talk.

"My name is Homa," she said. "I escaped

from Mazar-e-Sharif just after the Taliban captured the city."

"The Taliban has captured Mazar!" Parvana exclaimed. "That can't be! My mother is there. My brother and sisters are there."

"The Taliban is in Mazar," Homa repeated. "They went from house to house, looking for enemies. They came to my house. They came right inside! They grabbed my father and my brother and took them outside. They shot them right in the street. My mother started hitting them, and they shot her, too. I ran back inside and hid in a closet. I was there for a long, long time. I thought they would kill me, too, but they were finished killing people at my house. They were busy killing at other houses.

"Finally I left the closet and went downstairs. There were bodies all over the street. Some soldiers drove by in a truck. They forbade us to move the bodies of our families, or even cover them up. They said we must stay inside.

"I was so scared they would come back for me! When it got dark, I ran outside. I ran from building to building, looking out for the soldiers. There were bodies everywhere. The wild dogs had started eating some of the bodies, so there were pieces of people on the sidewalks and in the streets. I even saw a dog carrying a person's arm in its mouth!

"I couldn't face anything else. There was a truck stopped on the street. Its motor was running. I jumped into the back and hid among the bundles. Wherever the truck was going, it couldn't be worse than where I was.

"We traveled a long, long time. When I finally got out, I was in Kabul. I went from the truck to the building where Parvana found me." Homa started to cry. "I just left them there! I left my mother and my father and my brother lying in the street for the dogs to eat!"

Mrs. Weera put her arms around Homa, but the girl could not be comforted. She cried until she collapsed into an exhausted sleep.

Parvana couldn't move. She couldn't speak. All she could do was picture her mother, sisters and brother, dead in the streets of a strange city.

"There's no evidence your family is hurt, Parvana," Mrs. Weera said. "Your mother is a smart, strong woman, and so is Nooria. We must believe they are alive. We must not give up hope!"

Parvana was fresh out of hope. She did what her mother had done. She crawled onto the toshak, covered herself with a quilt and resolved to stay there forever.

For two days she stayed on the toshak. "This is what the women in our family do when we're sad," she said to Mrs. Weera.

"They don't stay there forever," Mrs. Weera said. "They get up again, and they fight back."

Parvana didn't answer her. She didn't want to get up again. She was tired of fighting back.

Mrs. Weera was gentle with her at first, but she had her hands full with Homa and her grandchild.

Late in the afternoon of the second day, Shauzia showed up at Parvana's door.

"I'm very glad to see you," Mrs. Weera said, nodding toward Parvana. They went out onto the landing to speak for a moment, out of Parvana's earshot. Then they came back in and, after fetching a couple of buckets of water, Shauzia sat down on the toshak beside Parvana.

She talked about ordinary things for awhile, how her sales had been, people she'd seen in the market, conversations she'd had with some of the tea boys and other working boys. Finally she said, "I don't like working alone. The marketplace isn't the same when you're not there. Won't you come back?"

Put to her like that, Parvana knew she could not refuse. She'd known all along that she would have to get up. She wasn't really about to stay on that toshak until she died. Part of her wanted to slip away from everything, but another part wanted to get up and stay alive and continue to be Shauzia's friend. With a little prodding from Shauzia, that was the part that won.

Parvana got out of bed and carried on as before. She did her work in the market, fetched water, listened to Mrs. Weera's stories and got to know Homa. She did all these things because she didn't know what else to do. But she moved through her days as though she were moving through an awful nightmare—a nightmare from which there was no release in the morning.

Then, late one afternoon, Parvana came home from work to find two men gently helping her father up the steps to the apartment. He was alive. At least part of the nightmare was over.

FIFTEEN

The man who came back from prison was barely recognizable, but Parvana knew who he was. Although his white shalwar kameez was now gray and tattered, although his face was drawn and pale, he was still her father. Parvana clung to him so tightly she had to be pulled away by Mrs. Weera so that her father could lie down.

"We found him on the ground outside the prison," one of the men who had brought him home said to Mrs. Weera. "The Taliban released him, but he was unable to go anywhere on his own. He told us where he lived, so my friend and I put him on our karachi and brought him here."

Parvana was down on the toshak with her father, clinging to him and weeping. She knew that the men stayed to tea, but it wasn't until they were getting up to leave, to make it back to their homes before curfew, that she remembered her manners.

She got to her feet. "Thank you for bringing my father back," she said.

The men left. Parvana started to lie back down beside her father, but Mrs. Weera stopped her. "Let him rest. There will be time to talk tomorrow."

Parvana obeyed, but it took days of Mrs. Weera's careful nursing before Father even started to get well. Most of the time he was too ill and weary to talk. He coughed a lot.

"That prison must have been cold and damp," Mrs. Weera said. Parvana helped her make a broth and fed it to her father hot, off a spoon, until he was able to sit up and eat.

"Now you are both my daughter and my son," Father said when he was well enough to notice her new appearance. He rubbed his hand over her cropped hair and smiled.

Parvana made many trips to the water tap. Father had been beaten badly, and the poultice bandages Mrs. Weera put over his wounds had to be changed and washed frequently. Homa helped, too, mostly by keeping Mrs. Weera's granddaughter quiet so Father could rest.

Parvana didn't mind that he was unable to talk right away. She was overjoyed just to have him home. She spent her days earning money, and her evenings helping Mrs. Weera. When her father felt better, she would read to him from his books.

Homa knew some English from studying it in school, and one day Parvana came home from work to hear Homa and Father talking English to each other. Homa hesitated a lot, but Father's words flowed smoothly into each other.

"Did you bring us home another educated woman today?" Father asked Parvana, smiling.

"No, Father," Parvana replied. "I just brought home onions." For some reason, everyone thought that was funny, and there was laughter in Parvana's home for the first time since her father's arrest.

One thing in her life had been repaired. Her father was home now. Maybe the rest of the family would come back, too.

Parvana was filled with hope. In the market she chased after customers just like the real boys did. Mrs. Weera suggested some medicine for Father, and Parvana worked and worked until she had earned the money to buy it. It seemed to help.

"I feel like I'm working for something now,"

she told Shauzia one day as they walked around looking for customers. "I'm working to get my family back."

"I'm working for something, too," Shauzia said. "I'm working to get away from Afghanistan."

"Won't you miss your family?" Parvana asked.

"My grandfather has started to look for a husband for me," Shauzia replied. "I overheard him talking to my grandmother. He said I should get married soon."

"Won't your mother stop him?"

"What could she do? She has to live with them. She has nowhere else to go." Shauzia stopped walking and looked at Parvana. "I *can't* be married! I *won't* be married!"

"How will your mother manage without you there? How will she eat?"

"What can I do?" Shauzia asked, the question coming out as a wail. "If I stay here and get married, my life will be over. If I leave, maybe I'll have a chance. There must be some place in this world where I can live. Am I wrong to think like this?" She wiped the tears from her face. "What else can I do?"

Parvana didn't know how to comfort her friend.

One day Mrs. Weera had a visitor, a member of the women's group who had just come out of Mazar. Parvana was at work, but Father told her about the visit that evening.

"A lot of people have fled Mazar," he said. "They are staying in refugee camps outside the city."

"Is that where Mother is?"

"It's possible. We won't know unless we go to the camps and look."

"How can we do that? Are you well enough to travel?"

"I will never be well enough," Father said, "but we should go anyway."

"When do we leave?" Parvana asked.

"As soon as I can arrange transport. Can you carry a message for me to the men who brought me home from prison? I think, with their help, we can be on our way in a couple of weeks."

Parvana had been wanting to ask her father something for awhile. "Why did the Taliban let you go?"

"I don't know why they arrested me. How would I know why they let me go?"

Parvana would have to be satisfied with that for an answer.

Her life was about to change again. She was surprised at how calm she felt. She decided it was because her father was back.

"We'll find them," Parvana said with complete confidence. "We'll find them and bring them home."

Mrs. Weera was going to Pakistan. "Homa will come with me. We'll put her to work there." They were going to link up with the members of the women's group who were organizing Afghan women in exile.

"Where will you stay?"

"I have a cousin in one of the camps," Mrs. Weera replied. "She has been wanting me to come and live with her."

"Is there a school there?"

"If there isn't, we'll start one. Life is very difficult for Afghans in Pakistan. There is a lot of work to do."

Parvana had an idea. "Take Shauzia with you!"

"Shauzia?"

"She wants to leave. She hates it here. Couldn't she go with you? She could be your escort!"

"Shauzia has family here. Do you mean to say she would just leave her family? Desert the team just because the game is rough?"

Parvana said no more. In a way, Mrs. Weera was right. That was what Shauzia was doing. But Shauzia was also right. Didn't she have a right to seek out a better life? Parvana couldn't decide who was more right.

A few days before they were to leave for Mazar, Parvana was sitting on her blanket in the marketplace when something hit her on the head. It was a tiny camel made out of beads. The Window Woman was still alive! She was all right, or at least well enough to let Parvana know she was still there. Parvana wanted to jump up and down and dance. She wanted to yell and wave at the painted window. Instead she sat quietly and tried to think of a way to say goodbye.

She was almost home that afternoon when she thought of a way.

Heading back to the market after lunch, she carefully dug up some wildflowers that were growing among the bombed-out ruins. She had seen them growing there in other years, and hoped she was right in thinking they were the kind that grew year after year. If she planted the flowers in the spot where she usually put her blanket, the Window Woman would know she wasn't coming back. The flowers would be something pretty to look at. She hoped they would make a good present.

In her spot in the market, Parvana dug up the hard soil first by pounding into it with her ankle. She used her hands, too, as well as a rock she found nearby.

The men and boys in the market gathered around to watch her. Anything different was entertainment.

"Those flowers won't grow in that soil," someone said. "There are no nutrients in it."

"Even if they grow, they will be trampled."

"The marketplace is no spot for flowers. Why are you planting them there?"

Through the voices of derision came another voice. "Do none of you appreciate nature? This boy has undertaken to bring a bit of beauty into our gray marketplace, and do you thank him? Do you help him?" An old man pushed his way to the front of the little gathering. With difficulty, he knelt down to help Parvana plant the flowers. "Afghans love beautiful things," he said, "but we have seen so much ugliness, we sometimes forget how wonderful a thing like a flower is."

He asked one of the tea boys hovering nearby for some water from the tea shop. It was fetched, and he poured it around the flowers, soaking the earth around them.

The plants had wilted. They didn't stand up properly.

"Are they dead?" Parvana asked.

"No, no, not dead. They may look scraggly and dying now," he said, "but the roots are good. When the time is right, these roots will support plants that are healthy and strong." He gave the earth a final pat, and Parvana and one of the others helped him up. He smiled once more at Parvana, then walked away.

Parvana waited by her flowers until the crowd had gone. When she was sure no one was watching, she looked up at the window and waved a quick goodbye. She wasn't sure, but she thought she saw someone wave back.

Two days later they were ready to leave.

They were going to travel by truck, just as the rest of the family had done.

"Am I traveling as your son or your daughter?" Parvana asked Father.

"You decide," he said. "Either way, you will be my little Malali."

"Look at what's here!" Mrs. Weera said. After making sure the coast was clear, she took several copies of Mother's magazine out from under her burqa. "Isn't it beautiful?"

Parvana flipped through the magazine quickly before hiding it again. "It's wonderful," she said.

"Tell your mother that copies are being sent out to women all over the world. She has helped to let the world know what is happening in Afghanistan. Be sure you tell her that. What she did was very important. And tell her we need her back, to work on the next issue."

"I'll tell her." She gave Mrs. Weera a hug. Both Mrs. Weera and Homa were wearing burqas, but she could tell by hugging them who was who.

It was time to leave. Suddenly, just as the truck was ready to pull out onto the road, Shauzia appeared.

"You made it!" Parvana said, hugging her friend.

"Goodbye, Parvana," Shauzia said. She handed Parvana a bag of dried apricots. "I'm leaving soon, too. I met some nomads who will take me to Pakistan as a shepherd. I'm not waiting until next spring. It would be too lonely here without you."

Parvana didn't want to say goodbye. "When will we see each other again?" she asked in a panic. "How will we keep in touch?"

"I've got it all figured out," Shauzia said. "We'll meet again on the first day of spring, twenty years from now."

"All right. Where?"

"The top of the Eiffel Tower in Paris. I told you I was going to France."

Parvana laughed. "I'll be there," she said. "We won't say goodbye, then. We'll just say so long for now."

"Until next time," Shauzia said.

Parvana hugged her friend one last time, then climbed into the truck. They waved to each other as the truck rolled away.

Twenty years from now, Parvana thought. What would happen in those twenty years?

Would she still be in Afghanistan? Would Afghanistan finally have peace? Would she go back to school, have a job, be married?

The future stretched unknown down the road in front of her. Her mother was somewhere ahead with her sisters and her brother, but what else they would find, Parvana had no idea. Whatever it was, she felt ready for it. She even found herself looking forward to it.

Parvana settled back in the truck beside her father. She popped a dried apricot into her mouth and rolled its sweetness around on her tongue. Through the dusty front windshield she could see Mount Parvana, the snow on its peak sparkling in the sun.

AUTHOR'S NOTE

Afghanistan is a small country in central Asia. It contains the Hindu Kush mountain range, fast-flowing rivers and golden deserts. Its fertile valleys used to produce an abundance of fruit, wheat and vegetables. Conquerors and explorers throughout history have seen Afghanistan as a gateway to the Far East.

Afghanistan has been at war since 1978, when American-backed fighters opposed the Soviet-backed government. In 1980, the Soviet Union invaded Afghanistan, and the war escalated, with both sides bombing and killing with modern weapons.

After the Soviets left in 1989, a civil war erupted, as various groups fought for control of the country.

Millions of Afghans became refugees, and many still live in huge camps in Pakistan and Iran. Many people have spent their whole lives in these camps. Millions have been killed, maimed or blinded.

Twenty years of war have also destroyed roads, bridges and waterways. Few people in Afghanistan have clean water to drink. Land mines were put by all the armies in farmers' fields, making it impossible to grow food there. As a consequence, many people die of hunger or from diseases caused by poor nutrition.

The Taliban militia, an Afghan army, took over control of the capital city of Kabul in September, 1996. They imposed extremely restrictive laws on girls and women. Schools for girls were closed down, women were no longer allowed to hold jobs, and strict dress codes were enforced. Books were burned, televisions smashed, and music in any form was forbidden. Since that time, the Taliban have conquered more and more of the country each year.

GLOSSARY

burqa - A long, tent-like garment, which the Taliban have decreed women must wear whenever they go outside. It covers them completely and even has a narrow mesh screen over the eyes.

chador - A piece of cloth worn by women and girls to cover their hair and shoulders. Girls wear this outside.

Dari - One of the two main languages spoken in Afghanistan.

Eid - A Moslem festival coming at the end of Ramadan, the month of fasting.

karachi - A cart on wheels, pushed by hand, used to sell things in the market.

kebab - Pieces of meat on a skewer, cooked over a fire.

land mine - A bomb planted in the ground, which explodes if it is stepped on.

nan - Afghan bread—flat, sometimes long and sometimes round.

pakul - A gray or brown woolen blanket shawl worn by Afghan men and boys.

Pashtu - One of the two main languages spoken in Afghanistan.

shalwar kameez - Long, loose shirt and trousers, worn by both men and women. Men's are all one color, with pockets in the side and on the chest. Women's are different colors and patterns, sometimes elaborately embroidered or beaded.

Soviets - The Soviet Union before its break-up, including Russia and other Communist countries.

Taliban - Members of the ruling party in Afghanistan.

toshak - A narrow mattress used in many Afghan homes instead of chairs or beds.